WHY ARE WE
SITTING HERE
UNTIL WE DIE?

WHY ARE WE SITTING HERE UNTIL WE DIE?

By
Mark T. Hancock
with Eva Marie Everson

Straight Street Books
Lighthouse Publishing of the Carolinas

WHY ARE WE SITTING HERE UNTIL WE DIE
BY MARK T. HANCOCK WITH EVA MARIE EVERSON

Published by Straight Street Books
an imprint of Lighthouse Publishing of the Carolinas
2333 Barton Oaks Dr., Raleigh, NC, 27614

ISBN: 978-1-946016-81-2
Copyright © 2019 by Mark T. Hancock with Eva Marie Everson
Cover design by Elaina Lee
Interior design by AtriTeX Technologies P Ltd.

Available in print from your local bookstore, online, or from the publisher at:
ShopLPC.com

For more information on this book and the author, visit www.MarkTHancock.com

Brought to you by the creative team at Lighthouse Publishing of the Carolinas
(LPCBooks.com): Eddie Jones, Cindy Sproles, Denise Loock, and Elaina Lee

Library of Congress Cataloging-in-Publication Data

Hancock, Mark T. with Everson, Eva Marie

Why Are We Sitting Here Until We Die/ Mark T. Hancock with Eva Marie Everson 1st ed.

Printed in the United States of America

If you're ready to find out how you can turn in your "donkey heads" and "dove droppings" (you'll have to read this book to discover what that means) for a medium-rare filet mignon with béarnaise sauce, then you have found the right book. Mark Hancock wants to help you find your cause and maximize your life. Mark's book will challenge you to the core, and it will equip you to be a true difference maker. Read this book. It's health food for the soul and your career path.

~Dr. Dennis Rainey
Co-founder
FamilyLife

Mark Hancock's book resonated with me so viscerally that I had a hard time putting it down. It paints a picture of how we, as believers, should live but, sadly, all too often don't. If you find yourself asking, "Is this all there is?" then read Mark's book—and take the risk of true living.

In 2015, I started living the life Mark's book describes. That year I responded to God's call and began a walk of faith. Looking back, what unsettles me now is realizing how easy it would've been to dismiss the call of God. Hidden in mundane ordinariness, I felt a subtle but unmistakable beckoning to something beyond what I thought I could do. I heeded the call, and my life has become an adventure of faith where I feel more alive than ever.

Be ready when God calls you for His assignment. To prepare you for a big thing, He may first call you to a small thing. But read Mark's book now so you won't miss His call.

~Robert McFarland
President, Transformational Impact LLC
Blogger-in-Chief, RobertMcFarland.net
Author of *Dear Boss: What Your Employees Wish You Knew*
and *Dear Employee: What Your Boss Wishes You Knew*

How do I measure success? Where is God calling me? Am I meeting my potential? What is my next challenge? This compelling book by Mark Hancock dares you to get off your keister and finally uncover answers to these critical life questions. For every authentic Christian, it's time to take a stand.

~Jay Payleitner
National speaker
Best-selling Author of
What If God Wrote Your Bucket List?
and *The Jesus Dare*

Mark Hancock leads a powerful ministry, standing in the gap of the war on boys. His new book grabs you by the chest and shakes you. Prepare to be enthralled, captivated, and convicted.

~Rick Johnson

Best-selling Author of *Better Dads, Stronger Sons* and *10 Things Great Dads Do*

Almighty God fuels much-needed courage when we see it in others who are willing to share their life and their story with us. Mark creatively does that in *Why Are We Sitting Here Until We Die?* He inspires me to listen and hear from God during this next season of life and to accept what He offers me.

~Brian Doyle

Founder and President of Iron Sharpens Iron

This book will capture the heart of any person looking to answer the age-old questions: What's my purpose / calling in God? And am I fulfilling my personal, God-ordained destiny, established before time began?

Mark approaches these critical questions from a brand-new direction, opening Scripture with amazing clarity and weaving biblical questions into our personal searches. Mark is an encourager by nature who knows discovering God's ultimate design for our lives is attainable. He gives concise examples and a path for discerning our calls, fine-tuning our spiritual ears to hear, and then being available for an amazing relationship with our heavenly Father.

We want to be Father Pleasers, which should always point the fruit of our lives and ministries to Jesus on the cross and that ramification for the world. Reconciling the lost to our Lord should be first and foremost in all we say and do.

This book will bring peace and confidence to all who are willing to ask the right questions about their destiny in Christ and then to implement the facts they encounter. This book is timely for both newbies and seasoned Christians who are sensing the possibilities of new ventures in their walks. Mark is gifted in challenging Christians to become all they are purposed to be in Christ. In business, as in life, following God's direction yields the highest returns.

~Tim Devore

Executive Coach and President

DevoreInc.com

Mark's book is clever and convicting. He weaves together ancient stories with today's realities. He has created a helpful resource for busy leaders like me. Whether you're on the fence or already charging into the battle, this book may be the guidance (and kick in the pants) you need. I appreciate Mark's candor and humor throughout. I highly recommend it.

~Kent Evans
Executive Director, Manhood Journey
and Author of *Wise Guys: Unlocking Hidden Wisdom from the Men around You*

Why Are We Sitting Here Until We Die? stings like a hard whack on the side of the head. Mark Hancock delivers a direct blow through storytelling that is captivating and hard hitting. His fresh and compelling exploration of what keeps us from wholeheartedly saying yes to God (no matter the cost) brings you to the end of yourself. This book awakened a deeper longing in me to "fill the frames of the images I was shaped for ..." I highly recommend you breathe deep, read this book, and start to live the life God has for you. The promise? No regrets!

~Tami Heim
President and CEO, Christian Leadership Alliance

TABLE OF CONTENTS

Bonus Content

ACKNOWLEDGMENTS

A special thanks to the love of my life, best friend, and wife of thirty years who encouraged me to take the first step and sign up for a writers conference. After you read the first page of the first draft, you said, "Honey! You're a writer!" I will never forget that. Without exception, you have encouraged me in faith to answer the call wherever that leads, and I can't imagine a better life partner. Thank you for adding to the depth of this work at every turn.

It is a joy to acknowledge the role Eva Marie Everson played in making this work a reality. Your commitment and immediate grasp of the message made you the perfect person to help carry this to completion. Thank you for believing in your—*ahem*—much, *much* younger brother.

Thank you to the awesome team at Lighthouse Publishing—Cindy Sproles, Denise Loock, and the rest of the crew helping this project get out of the gate!

Thank you to my pastor, Joe Putting, who generously supported and encouraged both my wife and me in our "leave the gate" adventures. You are a living example of the principles in this book and have inspired countless others to do big things for God. (Readers can find a sliver of his story in these pages and catch a glimpse of a man who loves the Kingdom more than his own castle. We need more like him.)

Heartfelt thanks to the men and women I've met around the globe who rise to answer the question and inspire the rest of us to do the same. And a Trailman's handshake to the thousands of Trail Life USA leaders across the country, many of whom left something sure for something risky that spoke to their heart.

And to Jesus, who leads the way out of bondage and mediocrity to a treasure that is beyond measure.

Mark T. Hancock

And now for my two cents: My heart smiled when Mark asked me if I would come alongside him in this project. I have long believed in his work and in his ministry, and I have seen and experienced firsthand the godliness that emanates from my friend. Thank you, Mark, for allowing your *much*, much older sister to come along for the ride.

Many thanks to the main man in my life, my husband and best friend, Dennis Everson. You put up with so much and allow so much because you see the importance of the work. With the exception of Christ living in me, your support is the only reason I can do what I do.

And to our Father in heaven, His Son beside Him—
in us and through us by the power of His Holy Spirit—
we praise You … we thank You … we love You forever.

Eva Marie Everson

For Luke and Logan
Two of the best men I know, fit for whatever adventure
awaits you and totally and completely loved:
city, gate, or treasure.
Dad

For Vonché
My special trailblazer and grandson extraordinaire.
I love you.
MiMi

The Power
of a Question

I believe that at the core of every man and woman a question waits to be answered—one that is God-placed and rises over the course of time. Then, when life adds its experiences, the question becomes a proclamation. The proclamation then finds a willing ear.

Or maybe a heart. Maybe yours.

Questions have a way of locating the lost (*Then the Lord God called to Adam and said to him, "Where are you?"*),[1] clarifying the critical (*"But who do you say that I am?"*),[2] and drawing out the crux of one's desire (*"Do you want to be made well?"*).[3]

When we're quiet, when we're seeking, or when we're caught in a tough spot, the question rises like the next speaker at a graduation and makes its solicitation.

My core question grabbed me in Ghana, Africa. A speaker whom I'd never heard stood and spoke the question from Scripture.

I was hooked.

I didn't know it at the time, but I'd reached a crossroad, and the question rose just in time. I felt like I was a graduating student, and this was my commencement address. But graduation from what? To what?

1

Our lives are full of crossroad experiences that provide opportunity to hear the core question and choose the course. God is sovereign in our lives, and He gives us a *narrow gate*[4] that we may choose to walk through.

In Africa, at one of many key points in my life, God spoke into my heart saying, "You've arrived at today with certain experiences, relationships, and lessons learned. This is a time to consider—will you rest in those? Or will you step forward into the next season, where you will be challenged with new opportunities?"

The core question became my narrow gate. By God's hand, it had swung open wide, but I had to choose whether I'd walk through it.

ARE YOU APPROACHING A CROSSROAD?

Maybe you wonder if there's something more. Your ideas have run their course, and you're not satisfied with where you find yourself. Perhaps you're in the midst of a great loss, and you lack the energy to move on; or you find yourself at a transition in life, and you wonder which way to turn. If so, this book may help you find direction.

Maybe you're a lifelong believer but you've lost your passion. Ordinary church life doesn't do it for you anymore. You ask yourself, *Is this all there is?* You feel called to something greater. You want to reignite a flame or to grab some inspiration for the next leg of the journey. Dreams or glimpses of what could've been are fading. But on their way out, they tug on a question. This book can help blow life back into embers grown cold, or it may give you the needed inspiration to reach for something more.

Maybe you're at the top of your game. You're of the breed that pursues a goal or a task 100 percent, but you want to stay on the cutting edge in pointing others to their destiny. You've answered the question, you're wide awake with the purpose of God for your life, and you want language for the answer. Perhaps this book can give you a metaphor that will not only complete the longing for you but also help you package your message so you may be the catalyst for a breakthrough for others.

The most important issue here is that you're bold enough to ask yourself the core question.

The source of what is, for our purposes, the overriding and title question of this book is from 2 Kings 7.

City under Siege

Here's the story:

Samaria, the capital of Israel, is under siege by the Syrian army. Samaria had provided a banquet for the Syrians—testament to its former wealth and ability to bless—but the Syrian army has sealed the city.

The siege has devastating effects. Scarcity of food is such that even a donkey's head is unaffordable for most citizens. Another food option is dove droppings. Some have even taken to boiling and eating their own children. The people are barely surviving. They have no real plan but cling to the hope that something—or someone—can bring change. Responding to a woman desperate for nourishment, the king himself proclaims, *"If the Lord does not help you, where can I find help for you?"* [5]

Pretty grim stuff.

Meanwhile, outside the entrance to the city, specifically at the gate, four lepers sit. And they are the heroes of our story. They have no illusions about the city's ability to provide for them and no real hope of surviving at the familiar place of the gate. And they know the Syrian army encamped out of sight is their sworn enemy. Surrender doesn't guarantee survival.

So the lepers ask the core question, *"Why are we sitting here until we die?"* [6]

Can you sense the power in their question? There's a deep-gut seriousness about the situation that springs to its feet and proposes *the* question of the moment. It's the core question that—if ignored—means the moment will pass unnoticed, and these four lepers (and ultimately the citizens of Samaria) will die in obscurity—overwhelmed not by a more powerful enemy but as a result of neglecting the question.

"Why are we sitting here until we die?"

So here you and I sit. What will we do with the question?

If I'd been one of the other three lepers, I'd have struggled for something to say. "What do you mean? Do you have a better idea?"

Or I might have said, "Leave the gate? You must be kidding me! Has the leprosy infected your brain?"

Perhaps I've become quite comfortable at the gate. I'm neither slave to the lack inside the walls or under immediate threat from the aggression of the Syrians. I'm biding my time, reluctant to push myself and make changes. After all, who'd expect anything more from me? I'm not a starving citizen of the city, but I'm not a bloodthirsty Syrian either. I am what I am. I'm a leper. I can ignore the question and accept that I'm dying at the gate, or I can engage the question and give it an honest appraisal.

ENGAGING THE QUESTION

This book is about engaging the question and taking the risk of living. It provides some scriptural strategies for getting us out of the city, away from the gate, and into the riches of our pursuit of God's promises.

In my years as a mental health counselor, I have often sat spellbound by the courage of regular folks who, when the core question rises, choose to embrace it in whatever form it takes, and then make both minor and major adjustments so they can fully live again.

In my ministry travels on almost every continent, I've been touched by the strength of good people in difficult circumstances who abandon the status quo, no matter how familiar, because they've awakened to their core question and dig deep to find the resolve to go forth and live. Sometimes with nothing of any value and no visible God-given abilities, they seize the question and set out, accomplishing mighty exploits for the sake of the kingdom. And in the pursuit, they find their greatest joy in fully living.

Over the past five years in leading Trail Life USA, I've walked with courageous men and women who left an established century-old organization to embrace a living ministry to men and boys. They found meaning in a Christ-centered, boy-focused calling to the outdoors.

I've also witnessed people who, although esteemed in their field or circle of influence, ignore or deflect the notion of something deeper, richer, or greater. They never leave the safety of the impoverished city or the security and anonymity of the gate. They've settled for their current state and, although alert to the realization that there may be more, decide it isn't worth it, or they lack the energy, vision, or—more likely—the (en)courage(ment) to go out. The gate is their grave; they just haven't stopped breathing yet.

"IF THEY KILL US, WE SHALL ONLY DIE"[7]

We pick up the story here:

The lepers decided to take their chances. At twilight they rose to go to the Syrian camp and discovered that the most incredible thing had happened: *"When they had come to the outskirts of the Syrian camp, to their surprise, no one was there."*[8] The big, bad Syrians were nowhere to be seen. And not only that, they'd left behind all their belongings: tents, horses, donkeys, food, drink, silver, gold, and clothing.

As it turned out, *the Lord had caused the army of the Syrians to hear the noise of chariots and the noise of horses—the noise of a great army.*[9] The Syrians had fled at twilight.

Needless to say, the lepers had a party. They went from tent to tent, eating and drinking and stashing treasure until guilt got the best of them and they decided to share their good news with the city. They were satisfied and Samaria was saved, thereby securing a future for the people of God.

Could it be that your breakthrough, your treasure, your fulfillment lies just over the horizon? Could it be God has already gone ahead to clear the way for your absolute purpose in Him? I doubt these lepers had any greater claim to fame than bringing this good news into the city.

Could there be such an opportunity for you?

Your greatest victory could be waiting one decision away, already delivered by a God who has gone before you.

But engaging your core question is not for the faint of heart. It takes courage to launch out. Explorers have to leave someplace familiar to go somewhere spectacular. Scary stuff. Can you imagine heading west from Spain or England? East through China? Into the atmosphere? North America, new trade routes, or the dark side of the moon—you've got to let go of the familiar to find the spectacular. You've got to leave the city or the gate to grab your treasure.

It takes courage to respond to the core question of your heart. I've purposed to help you identify and enhance skills you may already have or to develop new skills that will aid in your journey.

Skills such as those found in Section One, *Discerning the Times*. If you're unsure you're under siege or hesitant to begin, this skill will equip you to evaluate your status and to make your move at the right time.

Section Two, *Finding the Cause*, will help you realize your readiness for the journey. Your role as an unlikely hero is central to God having the victory. You are not limited in Him.

Section Three, *Taming the Power of Influence*, will address your stewardship of the things to come. Some who've gone before you wasted the treasure on themselves or, even worse, buried it. God will use you as people are drawn to what you've found. These practical guidelines will help you make the ideal real.

Now to the quest. For some reason, you're reading this book. The core question has risen in your heart. You can lift your eyes from the scarcity of the city, take your hand off the security of the gate, and take a step toward the Syrian camp and the treasure that waits.

Will you take the journey?

Don't worry. You're not alone. Just as with each of the lepers, there are *Three* that go with you.

You can do this. If you're willing, God will make you able.

Section One

DISCERNING THE TIMES

And they rose at twilight to go to the camp of the Syrians; and when they had come to the outskirts of the Syrian camp, to their surprise no one was there. For the Lord had caused the army of the Syrians to hear the noise of chariots and the noise of horses—the noise of a great army; so they said to one another, "Look, the king of Israel has hired against us the kings of the Hittites and the kings of the Egyptians to attack us!" Therefore they arose and fled at twilight, and left the camp intact—their tents, their horses, and their donkeys—and they fled for their lives.

2 KINGS 7: 5–7

Chapter 1

CITY OR GATE?
DISCERNING YOUR PLACE

SIEGE-DWELLERS

The question asked inside the city under siege is quite different from the question the lepers asked at the gate, but it's equally revealing:

And there was a great famine in Samaria; and indeed [the Syrian army] besieged it until a donkey's head was sold for eighty shekels of silver, and one-fourth of a kab of dove droppings for five shekels of silver.[10]

Donkey head and dove droppings? What a diet! And the price is exorbitant. If this happened today and in our country, the price for donkey head would run about four hundred dollars, a pint of dove droppings about twenty-five dollars. Give or take a shekel and a kab. But more shocking than this, Scripture shares an account of mothers who were willing to boil their children for food.[11]

Hello? Is anybody in the city paying attention?

13

Before the lepers launched out, the prophet Elisha declared to the king, *"Tomorrow about this time a seah of fine flour shall be sold for a shekel and two seahs of barley for a shekel, at the gate of Samaria."*[12] To the city-dwellers and leaders, that was an outlandish declaration.

Any reasonable citizen would realize that twenty-five dollars buys a pint of dove poop today, and yet the prophet claims that tomorrow thirty-five quarts of flour can be bought for the same amount. So, the citizen would say, "Things are going to be a lot better. I'm on board with you, Elisha. No more donkey head for me, no more dove droppings, no more boiling the kids—this is great news."

But the king's officer responds with a question that lacks faith in a promise that speaks directly to the needs of the city. The officer mocks the prophet by asking, *"Look, if the Lord would make windows in heaven, could this thing be?"*[13]

The officer pays a great price for his doubt. Not only does he not eat of the increase, but his life is taken also.

This is the question of the siege-dweller: *"Could this thing be?"* Or, better said: "Does God do what He says? Can He be trusted? Is trusting Him worth it?"

We can easily scoff at these words, but how much of the cynical siege-dweller lives in us? How often do we respond to the promises of God with a question of disbelief or an attitude that mocks His greatness?

What makes it so difficult for us to believe? How can we be so married to a lifestyle that lacks the fullness our heart longs for and the Word promises and not see the same potential for us that He sees in us?

What is it about siege-dwelling that keeps us under siege?

ANATOMY OF A SIEGE-DWELLER

When we are siege-dwellers, we settle. We defend the status quo. Our own stubborn thinking binds us to the siege and limits our potential in God. It keeps us from believing or expecting that anything better exists beyond the walls that have become so familiar yet so confining. "Could this thing be?" is our response to news that there is more beyond our walls.

We compare ourselves to other siege-dwellers instead of to who we should be, using our restricted physical senses as gauges of our status.

Years ago, I partnered with some pastors in a well-developed Asian nation, discussing ideas for church growth and opportunities for impacting one of the world's leading cultures with the dynamics of successful Christian living. When provided with some ideas for how to increase his congregation's impact on the capital-city neighborhood, a pastor responded, "We couldn't possibly do that. The other churches would see us as prideful and attempt to make us fail."

Have you ever heard of the analogy "we can be like crabs in a bucket"? Well, I've seen it—with actual crabs. If you put live crabs in a bucket, they'll try to escape using each other as leverage and claw-holds. No one escapes. Any crab nearing the top of the bucket is pulled back down by the crabs below.

This is the mind-set of the siege-dweller.

DONKEY HEAD

When we willingly live under siege, our expectations are low, our values distorted. As our common distortions are challenged, we become critical of those who try to escape. We resist change. Under siege, donkey head becomes a central part of our diet. Consuming the head of a stubborn beast of burden then begins to mess with our own head. Maybe we *are* what we eat.

Our limited-living saps strength from any God-given mandate and robs us of our God-given identity. The walls of our city become barriers built of uncertainty and the unknown. We forget that our faith, like a ladder, needs something against which to lean to reach its full height.

Recently, my family went on a trip to Zion National Park, Bryce Canyon, and the Grand Canyon, which are all part of the Colorado plateau. The floor of Bryce is at the altitude of the heights of Zion, and the floor of Zion is at the altitude of the heights of the Grand

Canyon. There is a stepping down as you travel south. The views are awe-inspiring in all three parks, but the perspectives are dramatically different.

Zion is seen primarily from the floor—looking up out of the canyon—while Bryce and the Grand Canyon are viewed looking down into the canyons. What a different perspective! Both vistas are majestic, but there is something different about a perspective that looks up and one that looks down. You may have to experience it to catch the difference, but siege-dwellers live as if they are constrained by the high walls of their circumstances while conquerors live as if they dwell above them.

Our donkey-headed stubborn thinking confirms the majesty of the walls that define our restrictive living while we forget that the obstacles give us something to climb. Uncertainty, like an opposing bookend, is the necessary counterpart to our faith. The lepers would have no triumph without the Syrians. The obstacle holds the treasure. The solution? Extend your ladder of faith. Lean it against the uncertainty.

DOVE DROPPINGS

Dove droppings aren't much better. How often we settle for something that was consumed elsewhere and dropped on us as second-generation sustenance. I'm thinking of our willingness to rely solely on pastors and teachers to consume the Word and drop on us what they've digested, instead of seeking the Source for ourselves. I'm thinking of our addiction to reality shows—which are far from real—at the cost of quality time living in or receiving revelation from God about the *real* reality.

Our contemporary Christian lives give us constant access—through radio, TV, the Internet, church services—to previously consumed revelation. We think it's food because it fills our stomachs, but the potent nutrition has already been extracted. The value is much greater when we consume it firsthand through vibrant, purposeful pursuit of revelation direct from the Source. The pursuit itself has great value, as the process brings us closer to the One who knows us best and loves us most.

Our fellowship and sustenance through and with other believers is essential—but it can't be primary. Our church services can be opportunities to receive and offer encouragement, to pray and worship together, to define and execute corporate strategy, but there is the danger of being lulled into a false sense of fullness. That's why many who attend faithfully are partially satisfied but not entirely strengthened. We become spectators.

For many, church attendance becomes the only expression of their faith. Like the siege-dweller, the routine is a poor substitute for the remarkable. It's no easy task to let go of our habitual diet, but the life we find in firsthand devotion and consumption brings a vibrancy and energy to all we do.

BOILED CHILDREN

The desperate mother in our story discovered that she'd sacrificed her baby in vain the previous day; her friend refused to reciprocate and boil her child today. The first woman's deal was falling apart. Her only option was an appeal to the king: beg him to force her friend to offer her child also. After all, it was only fair. She gave her heritage; her friend should too.

Under siege, the precious lives of children lose any value beyond what they can do for the adults. Look at the last fifty years or so of cultural change in America. Sweeping decisions and shifts in attitudes toward abortion, divorce, marriage, sexual orientation, and gender-blurring—all without regard to how the changes affect children. We weren't paying attention to them when we legalized abortion, normalized divorce, or redefined marriage and human sexuality. Siege-dwellers turn inward at the cost of the next generation.

In a self-centered siege mentality, we lose the next generation because we've lost our passion for living. If we don't demonstrate hope to the next generation by living in pursuit of something greater, we condemn them to something less than what we've experienced because our expectations affect theirs. We model how to hope (or not to hope).

Generational degeneration occurs when passion isn't passed on. And this inheritance is only received through direct observation. Our children must see us living vibrant lives in pursuit of God's treasure and His interests, or they'll be consumed by our lack of passion.

What about you? Are you a siege-dweller—constrained to the city? If so, there's hope. God wants to save the city.

And maybe He wants to use you.

STOP, SURVEY, SET THE COURSE

I'm not sure when or from whom my wife and I learned this exercise, but it has become so much a part of our lives that it now seems more automatic than intentional. That's ironic because the intent is to avoid the automatic, the status quo, and the ordinary.

We call it Stop, Survey, and Set the Course.

We invoke this occasionally to make sure our lives haven't found a rut and that we're pursuing the plan God has for our lives in an active, meaningful way. I love the old saying, "A rut is just a grave with both ends kicked out of it." The words speak for themselves. The last thing we want is to be "the walking dead."

20

So first, we Stop.

In life's busyness, the crowd gathering around us, and the noise of our culture, we often forget to stop and take a break. So my wife and I take a day or two, maybe an afternoon, or as little as an hour together. We purposely unplug and clear out the cobwebs. We position ourselves to hear each other and to hear the voice of God through each other.

And then we move to the second step, Survey, by turning that break into something more than an escape. We turn it into an intentional, fearless review of what we're doing. Are we in God's plan? Is there eternal significance to what we're putting our hands to? Is it good for God? For our family? For our community? For people beyond that community?

Finally, we Set the Course. This is where the tough questions are asked and answered. What will we do with what we've heard and noticed during the Survey stage? This is the gutsy, full-on, step-up-to-the-plate part of living that makes life full.

We've left careers, started businesses, enrolled in universities, and ministered to the homeless and hopeless. We've opened our hearts and home to countless youth, college students, married couples, missionaries, and foster kids. We homeschooled our sons. We traveled all over the world to help bring the good news of the gospel, encourage believers, and set up events for an international ministry. We've been intentional with our lives, our days, our energy, and our finances. Serving and leading, we've done our best to cooperate with the seasons ordained and authored by God. Sometimes leaving a job or a church. One time leaving the place we called home for twenty-six years with our two teenage sons to move states away to answer the call as we knew we should. I wrote this book. Every significant decision because of these Stop, Survey, and Set the Course moments.

I don't have specific Scripture for this, but I can tell you it has borne fruit in our lives and the lives, presumably, of others. And the adventures with God have been thrilling, fostering a relationship with Him that's alive, relevant, and head-over-heels full of love.

Nothing like that of a siege-dweller.

LIFE AT THE GATE

Under the influence of the city but on the fringes lives the gate-dweller.

It's unclear why the lepers were at the gate. It was common for lepers to be cast out of the city (although Scripture is unclear whether they actually suffered from leprosy or some other disease). Perhaps they weren't welcome in the city for another reason. Or perhaps they grew tired or bored and wanted something different but safe.

What does it mean to be stuck at the gate? On the outside looking in, unengaged in life either inside the city or outside its walls?

I've found myself at the gate looking in. I don't fit in the city. I can see that there's no longer anything there for me. The price exacted for a scrap of food is exorbitant, and I certainly don't want to raise my kids in that place. Not only that, but my occasional musings about something greater aren't embraced by city-folk, and I've lacked the courage to leave the gate to pursue something else.

The gate is a barren place. The call of God or the responsibility for living fully makes it impossible to stay at this place of indecision and complacency. We can fault others for not joining with us or for not making a way for us, but, ultimately, we will stand before God to give an account of our choices. Will He accept our gutless justification?

The city has vision-blocking walls. The gate has a hopeless rut.

But the gate was never meant to be my—or your—dwelling place. It's a place of coming and going. The lepers discussed their options and concluded they all ended in death. So what's the point? Die here or die there.

Much of our lives are lived in routine. If our intentional actions were as regular as our everyday thoughtless habits, we'd be powerhouses for God. But at the gate, we're not. We're invisible to the city and inconsequential to the enemy. We pretend to live.

Maybe we take some kind of solace in the relative safety, but what of our future? What of the destiny, purpose, and plan God intended for us?

Jesus speaks to our condition at the gate when He shares the parable of the talents.[14] The origin of our word *talent*, in the sense of ability, comes from this Scripture verse. Clearly, Jesus expects us to invest what we've been given to produce for the kingdom, not to squander it or to secure a place for ourselves. Gate-dwellers withhold and bury what has so graciously been invested in them. They are free from the city, but what does one do with such freedom?

Like the lepers, risk it.

A component of nearly every victory we see in God's Word is risk. Abraham on Mount Moriah. Moses before Pharaoh. Esther in front of her husband, the king. David in the face of Goliath. Gideon with his 300 soldiers. God gave these people the choice of staying at the gate or launching out.

I don't know about you, but I dread the thought of standing before God with some lame excuse for why I didn't pursue everything He delivered to me—and the city. How many cities full of people have been lost because a gate-dweller didn't have the guts to get out of the rut and pursue?

And all this when, over the horizon—if we could believe what God says and be bold enough to pursue it—are all His promises. An abundant life,[15] fruitful,[16] purposeful, and real. Life that is *exceedingly abundantly above all that we ask or think, according to the power that works in us.*[17]

What about you?

Do you cower in the city? Do you dig in at the gate?

Or do you venture out and take your chances with the Syrian army?

Chapter 2

UNDERSTANDING THE TIMES

Sitting in the passenger seat of a pastor's car in Accra, Ghana, I turned to his assistant, John, in the back seat, a man who faithfully accompanied his pastor everywhere he went. John rarely spoke but was quick to carry a Bible or to screen a cell phone call for his pastor.

After turning and engaging eye contact, I asked, "John, what are you going to do with this life God has given you?"

His jaw dropped. Then, using an unearned title he insisted I carry, he responded, "Dr. Mark, an angel came to me in a dream several weeks ago—before I met you—and told me that a white man would be coming to ask me that question. Since then I have been searching diligently for my purpose, understanding that it is much greater than I thought and that now is the time to pursue it."

I don't believe in coincidence. Scripture implies there is a divine order that includes divine timing orchestrated by an Almighty God who is committed to securing His created beings as partners to secure His creation for His glory.

That core question, asked at that time, in that setting, took on a significance that may have been missed in any other case. It was the beginning of John's leaving the gate. I hear from him on occasion. His story continues to unfold while I am further convinced that we must be sensitive to the wisdom of God in whatever form He reveals it.

But how will you know if your question is for this time?

SONS OF ISSACHAR

David's army at Hebron was growing by leaps and bounds as the tribes sent men of war *to turn over the kingdom of Saul to him, according to the word of the Lord.*[18]

Thousands of men became members of David's army, men described as:

- Armed with bows, using both the left hand and the right hand to hurl stones and shoot arrows with the bow
- Men whose faces were like the faces of lions and were as swift as gazelles on the mountain
- Valiant
- Mighty men of valor, famous men

- Fit for war

- Loyal

- Expert in war

- Stouthearted men who could keep ranks

- Men who could keep battle formation

- Men with shield and spear[19]

Can you picture these thousands—tens of thousands—gritty, scarred, and battle-hungry men converging on Hebron to make David king? You can almost smell the sweat and sense the zeal, angst, and expectation. A hair-trigger, powder-keg crush of men looking for a reason to demonstrate their allegiance. They were wound up tight like a spring and compressed into a geographic area not fit for their numbers or mettle. What—or who—could temper such a gathering?

In the midst of this crowd, we find the sons of Issachar, *men who had understanding of the times, to know what Israel ought to do, 200 chiefs and all their kinsmen under their command.*[20]

UNDERSTANDING OF THE TIMES

These men were knowledgeable in interpreting the weather, the signs, the seasons, the political climate. Their understanding and experience with the interplay of those elements made them crucial to David's cause. In this conquest and coronation, God would gather both the grit of the warrior and the wisdom of understanding men to secure the kingdom.

These elements are not exclusive, but complementary. And they live in us.

And from the days of John the Baptist until now the kingdom of heaven suffers violence, and the violent take it by force.[21] *Therefore be wise as serpents and harmless as doves.*[22]

To lay claim to what God has set before us, we must be prepared to be both forceful and wise. To honor God with these traits requires a heart like David's with militant strength to face the lion, the bear, or the giant—and prudent wisdom to restrain from killing Saul.

We are so far from overplaying our hand that we are much more likely to fall short because of too little grit than too little restraint. My sense is that we in the church are educated beyond our obedience and that restraint, though necessary, isn't the missing ingredient. Our politically correct culture (and some of our church culture) has turned us into tame sycophants, courtiers, and attendants rather than pioneers, pathfinders, and persuaders.

THE TEST OF WISDOM

We don't need more knowledge and understanding to act. We have plenty of Bible studies, devotionals, accountability groups, and self-help Christianity. What we desperately need is God's wisdom so we can properly administrate the strength He has invested in us.

Even with all that is invested in us—the greatness of *the Spirit of Him who raised Jesus from the dead* [23]—we must be able to understand the times and to be open to godly counsel. Why? Because our ignorance can cause us to do the wrong thing at the wrong time or for the wrong reason.

The disciples learned that lesson when Jesus asked them, *"Children, do you have any fish?"* [24] They'd been throwing nets out into the Sea of Galilee all night but had caught nothing. Going through the motions. Net in. Net out. Nothing. Repeat.

Almost like our Samarian siege-dwellers.

But when Wisdom spoke, they reconsidered what they'd been doing. They didn't recognize Jesus, but His question opened their hearts to hear His instruction: *"Cast the net on the right side of the boat, and you will find some."* [25]

And they did. A miracle catch! Wisdom prevailed, and the disciples were rewarded—both with the miracle catch and with the revelation that Jesus stood in their midst.

There is an order to the right things of God.

Time. Wisdom. The order of right things. As His ambassadors, it falls to us, like the sons of Issachar, to discern the times and to seek God's help in discerning our heart toward what He's doing in our midst.

Understanding the times means we can be empowered by God's Spirit to evaluate the season in light of what God is saying to us. For example, after Noah and his family emerged from the ark, the Lord said to Himself, *"While the earth remains, seedtime and harvest, cold and heat, winter and summer, and day and night shall not cease."*[26]

Seedtime and harvest. This is the way of the whole earth. Seasons are important. Proper timing is vital.

THE GOD WHO GOES BEFORE YOU

The pesky Philistines were at it again. Another raid on the Valley of Rephaim, the valley running southwest from Jerusalem to the Valley of Elah, where, years before, young David had defeated the infamous giant Goliath.

What was David, now king, to do? He had already whooped them once (my translation of KJV *smote*) and here they come again.

David inquired again of God, and God said to him, "You shall not go up after them; circle around them, and come upon them in front of the mulberry trees. And it shall be, when you hear a sound of marching in the tops of the mulberry trees, then you shall go out to battle, for

God has gone out before you to strike the camp of the Philistines." So David did as God commanded him, and they drove back the army of the Philistines from Gibeon as far as Gezer.[27]

God instructed David to wait for a sound. *Faith comes by hearing.*[28] When the task is clear, the reason pure, and our ears open to God's direction, we'll know the time to launch out.

Moses had that sense of timing. He left Egypt before facing a heap of trouble[29] and changed his course when he heard from a burning bush. In a psalm that acknowledges the workings of God in men's lives over the course of time, he wrote, *Teach us to number our days, that we may gain a heart of wisdom.*[30]

ORIENTATION VS. LOCATION

Let's look back to the lepers in the story of the city under siege. What made the timing right?

*They rose **at twilight** to go to the camp of the Syrians.*[31] Why twilight? Why didn't they rise at morning or at the third hour or some other time? Why is the Bible so specific about the time of day?

Second Kings 7:7 gives us a hint: *Therefore [the Syrian army] arose and fled **at twilight**, and left the camp intact—their tents, their horses, and their donkeys—and they fled for their lives.*

The question that prompted the lepers to leave the gate and the sound that scattered the Syrian soldiers had been perfectly orchestrated. Had the lepers left any sooner, they probably would've been slaughtered by their enemy. Any later, and the food would've been spoiled and plundered. Or perhaps they would've been too weak from hunger.

In the parable of the prodigal son, the son exclaims, in an epiphanic moment, *"How many of my father's hired servants have bread enough and to spare, and I perish with hunger!"* [32] It's not phrased in many translations as a question, but it seems like one to me. This revelation emerging at that time led him to do the right thing.

And then an interesting thing happens, which re-inforces the at-twilight moment we explored with the lepers. So *[the prodigal] arose and came to his father. But when he was still a great way off, his father saw him and had compassion, and ran and fell on his neck and kissed him.* [33]

Did you catch the beginning of the second sentence? *When he was still a great way off.* It seems that at the moment the prodigal rose to the question and oriented himself to his goal, his father ran to him.

As with the lepers and the prodigal, when we rise to the question that arises in us, the Father moves on our behalf. I'm not sure if their action prompted God's, or if God's action prompted theirs, but the point is the same. *To everything there is a season, a time for every purpose under heaven.* [34]

Some versions of the Bible use *activity* rather than *purpose*. That activity—or purpose—includes yours.

To understand the times, we must hear the instruction of the Lord. Whether our signal is as clear as the sound of marching in the trees, as gentle as a still small voice, as wise as the counsel of a godly advisor, or as insistent as a question rising in our heart, we can recognize that God is prompting us to orient ourselves—at this time—to the victory He has secured for us. The prompting becomes more apparent with time, but our orientation—our standing and facing the right way—becomes more critical than our location and releases His power.

There is a quickening that brings life to the action. When we wait at rest, He leads us in His paths ... *for His name's sake.*[35]

The world needs something real, and it doesn't come from additional programs or a bigger budget or the next great revelation from Scripture. What the world needs comes from orienting ourselves the same way as Abraham, Moses, David, Elijah, the lepers, and so many others did. They went before us to set the example of response to God's leading at the right time, tempered by wisdom, counsel, and a bold conviction to see the manifestation of a promise from God.

If we want to see revival, deliverance, healing, and miraculous provision, we can tune in, hear God's directives, and orient ourselves to see the victory.

Our part is to respond to God at the proper time and to rise to pursue the victory He has already attained for us. The victories in the Bible came about when someone rose at the right time, oriented in the right direction.

Your God-implanted question is guaranteed to bring God-intended glory. This is how we partner with Him—by orienting ourselves to His purpose.

"THE KINGDOM OF HEAVEN IS AT HAND"

These words of Jesus found in Matthew 3:2, Matthew 4:17, and Mark 1:15 didn't seem to fit in their day and time. Where were the warriors? Where was the army that would deliver the people of God from Roman occupation? Kingdom at hand? You're kidding, Jesus. Right?

As with David, Moses, the lepers (and so many others), it takes a hearing ear—not seeing eyes—to experience God's presence in the present. He isn't a God who set history in motion, then abandoned it to its own devices. He is more involved than that. Neither is He a God who regularly interferes in the physical realm to reorder things in His favor. He's much more relational than either of those extremes.

Whispering, prompting, and revealing His purposes in secret to those who have ears to hear, He is a king directly and intimately involved in His kingdom

36

through His subjects. He is a God who is very present in the present—in and through His followers, co-laboring in kingdom work.

Keep in mind, though, that *kingdom* is a loaded word. My wife and I attended a public prayer meeting in Orlando a few years ago. One pastor prayed from the platform, "Forgive us for being so busy building our castles that we have failed to build the kingdom." I'm not sure if anyone else heard what we heard, but his words pierced our hearts.

Are you building your castle or His kingdom? That changes everything. It changes the way we view ourselves and the call He may have on our lives. Many leaders ask for help in building their castles. Indeed, we can fall prey to castle-building ourselves. But it's a kingdom-call when we look to see where God is doing something and join Him there rather than entreating Him to join us in building our castle. Kingdom work is eternal work. Kingdom work puts others first. Kingdom work is less concerned with receiving credit ourselves and more concerned with bringing glory to God. It's work outside the walls of our castles.

Rare is the ministry leader who asks, "How can I help you fulfill your call?" rather than "Will you come help me fulfill my vision?" But they are out there. Listen for them. Look for them. Become one of them.

If we listen, we'll hear God's call to kingdom work. In a still small voice, in a thunderous clap, in a rustling of the trees, in the voice of His counsel, in His Word, in a question that rises from within or without. In a question that calls us beyond ourselves and our own castle to a treasure outside our walls. The kingdom is at hand when we stand in response to a sound.

At the sound, we aren't waiting on an invasion— we *are* the invasion. This clearly puts the responsibility on us. We'll talk a lot more about this in chapter 7, but God wants to move in the now. His presence is in the present—through you.

What core question has God planted in your heart? Is it the city question—*could this thing be?* Is it the gate question—*why are we sitting here until we die?* Or is it something else? Deep and resonant in your spirit, what are you hearing? Is it time to pursue?

The question is evidence that the Father has something in mind for you—that your deliverance or treasure or promise or dream stands ready to be released at your moment of rising.

And rising means leaving the gate.

Chapter 3

WHY LET GO OF THE GATE?

A t this moment, I'm writing in a café filled with people tending to plates abundant with food. The room is tastefully decorated, the chairs comfortable, and the temperature regulated. I have Wi-Fi, and beautiful classical music sets an ambience for my words to flow.

In our western affluence and comfort—when it's possible we're actually full of donkey head, dove droppings, or boiled children—what awakens us to the need that surrounds us and, in some cases, indwells us?

Grave circumstances opened the minds of the lepers to the possibility of something better than what they had at the gate of a city under siege, but what would inspire *us* to let go of our gate? We can sit where we are, doing what we're doing, or we can listen inward to a question rising in us. We can openly consider the possibility that there is a dream waiting to be fulfilled, a cause waiting to be acted upon, or a purpose waiting to be realized.

WHEN FEAR SLEEPS IN

When we accept there are great things God can do through us, we live beyond the ordinary. God can triumph through us, because that is where faith prevails. *There* we live beyond our own strength, experience, and intellect. There we fully trust in Him. We are (thankfully) out of our minds.

But in our minds, in the day-to-day of siege-dwelling, we are unaware that we have taken ourselves prisoner and enlisted Fear as our warden. Fear patrols the hall, keeping us captive and restricted to our natural state, where we surround ourselves with the familiar to keep the unknown at bay.

In this state we live. Not in cells deprived of luxury, but in lives stocked with amenities that appease: security, safety, certainty, and their likely by-products. The stuff we like—our financial plan, our insurance, our cable, our pension, our familiar acquaintances, our predictable outcomes—adorns the walls of our safe lives.

We submit to Fear willingly for a reason: it lets us live where we are. Without challenge. Without the risk that accompanies change (and vice versa).

But also without a complete victory.

What if, one day, Fear sleeps in? What if the cell door is left unlocked and we can access the extraordinary unrestricted by Fear? Will we then leave the cell? Will we leave the gate?

I love the question, "What would you do if you had everything you needed to do what God has called you to do?" People give all kinds of answers. But the one that makes the most sense to me is, "Exactly what I'm doing now." When it comes to accomplishing what God has called us to do, there is no lack. We have everything we need to fulfill His call to kingdom work. We should always be able to answer that question with confidence: "I have everything I need to do what God has called me to do."

Leaving the security of the gate may be essential to experiencing the greater purposes of God. So, what if our hesitation—or outright refusal—to let go is the reason the abundance we dream about is not the abundance we experience?

"Is There Not a Cause?"

The lines were drawn.

The Philistines encroached on Judean lands, encamped between Sochoh and Azekah. Attack was impending but delayed, perhaps because of the difficulty of moving their war chariots through the steep, rocky ravine that runs through the middle of the Valley of Elah.

Saul and the men of Israel cowered in the valley waiting for the inevitable as the Philistines' champion, the giant Goliath, presented Himself for forty days—morning and evening—looking for a fight. Enforcing the rule of Fear.

David, sent to the battlefront by his father to bring supplies to his brothers engaged in the standoff, observed the situation. He asked what would be done for the man who accepted the giant's challenge, which brought a harsh rebuke from his brother:

> *"Why did you come down here? And with whom have you left those few sheep in the wilderness? I know your pride and the insolence of your heart, for you have come down to see the battle."*
>
> *And David said, "What have I done now? Is there not a cause?"* [36]

David saw something the others didn't see and was bold enough to dream out loud, recognizing that the cause was such that God's provision for victory was guaranteed. If you spent any time at all in Sunday school and church as a youngster (or an adult), you probably know the rest of the story. David picked up five stones from the dry riverbed, put one in his slingshot, hurled it toward the laughing giant ... and, as the children's song says, "the giant came tumbling down."

In the midst of our agreeable lives, we'd be wise to carry David's question in our heart: *Is there not a cause?*

The enemy has mastered complacency, discouragement, and fear, using them as effectively today as he did against Saul and his men. But the right question asked with the right motive engages our passion, ignites our courage, disperses our fears, and prepares us for the victory.

Sometimes, however, even the right question asked with the wrong motive can give the answers we need. Here's an example: Centuries after David killed Goliath, David's descendent—God's Son—stood in hot dispute with the Jewish leaders of His day.

He said to them, *"And you shall know the truth, and the truth shall make you free."*

The leaders reminded Jesus that they were not slaves; therefore, they said, *"How can You say, 'You will be made free?'"*

Wrong motive and yet still the right answer. Not only for their un-listening ears, but for our listening ears: *"If the Son makes you free, you shall be free indeed."*[37]

Christ is the Great Liberator, which means Fear has no real power over us. As the psalmist so powerfully penned: *The Lord is on my side; I will not fear. What can man do to me?*[38]

David didn't allow Fear to stop him from killing the giant. Jesus didn't allow Fear to stop him from facing the cantankerous leaders of His day. They both saw what needed to be done—what needed to be said—and they acted.

WHAT INSPIRES US TO ACTION?

The earthly ministry of Jesus had reached a critical point. Today we'd say His ministry had gone viral, with news of the dead being resurrected, the sick being healed, and the wisdom of His words creating an attraction beyond what He, as an individual, could control. He sought refuge. A little peace and solitude. Some time to gather His thoughts. His bearings.

But once again, the crowds found Him.

Luke's gospel seems particularly attuned to this. The physician knew how this worked. His own vocation was dependent on his ability to help people. His account records Jesus' miracles: healing the withered, feeding the hungry, and raising the dead. Luke knew the desperate need of the people and the attention the stories of this Great Healer would attract, so he tells us of the multitudes, the swarms of needy folks, the fame abroad, the escape to preach from a boat or to retire to the wilderness, the crossing of the lake to pursue the demoniac, the virtue that flowed as Jesus *healed them all*.[39]

And then a shift. The significance of this transfer may be lost because the gospels continue to accentuate the work done by Jesus, but something changed:

Then [Jesus] called His twelve disciples together and gave them power and authority over all demons, and

44

*to cure diseases. He sent them to preach the kingdom of
God and to heal the sick.*[40]

Wait a minute. They were being *sent*. Independent
from Him. To other places. But with His power and
authority.

Jesus, recognizing the need to overcome the physical restrictions of His one physical body, introduced
the disciples (and us) to the concept of sanctioned authority.

SANCTIONING, MASTERY, AND PURPOSE

Contemporary business management theory is discovering that sanctioned authority—in the sense of allowing a person to move independently with equal power,
compounded by mastery and purpose—is one of the
greatest inspirational elements of significant personal
action. When people are given permission to exercise
authority (sanctioning), achieve mastery, and encounter purpose, they are inspired to action. More so than
by a promise of reward or a threat of punishment.

Jesus knew this. He understood that we want to
feel empowered to move with His authority toward
meaningful goals. But more than moving with His authority, we want to move with the hope of mastering
the goals and thus realizing a purposeful mission.

He entrusted His disciples—present and future—
with His authority. The disciples were encouraged to

leave their own gate, of sorts, to see the same treasure manifest in their presence that they had, up to this point, only seen in His.

In addition to inspiring us to walk in the same authority He had, Jesus set before the disciples (and us) the possibility of doing greater works. He opened the gate to permit us to master what He had done through the same Spirit He had accessed.[41] *"Most assuredly, I say to you,"* He said to them, *"he who believes in Me, the works that I do he will do also; and greater works than these he will do, because I go to My Father."*[42]

The apostle John tells us that Jesus was manifested for three primary reasons:

1) to destroy the works of the Enemy[43]

2) to cause sin to have no effect[44] and

3) to restore the broken relationship with the Creator/Father[45]

As His ambassadors, with His authority, that is our purpose toward others.[46] With David, we can ask, "Is there not a cause?" and dress with our flesh the dream God has placed in our heart.

When the need is unmistakably placed before us, we can hear His voice.

Years ago, I attended a gathering of 22,000 young people in Atlanta. In the course of three days, these young men and women contributed over $1.3 million to humanitarian causes around the world.[47] Something (or Someone) spoke to them, and they were inspired to rise in response to a need greater than their own. Is it possible that the first step toward receiving His inspiration to act is tuning ourselves to the voice of the One who has a purpose for us?

Jesus said, *"He who enters by the [gate] is the shepherd of the sheep. To him the [gatekeeper] opens, and the sheep hear his voice; and he calls his own sheep by name and leads them out. And when he brings out his own sheep, he goes before them; and the sheep follow him, for they know his voice."*[48]

We believe it is important to act. We cannot deny what we see or hear about the tremendous need for our action. Our faith compels us. But what will inspire us to act on this awareness? What thoughts will embolden us to let go of the gate?

Consider the following truths.

First, God's plan depends on us. Do you trust Him? You should. He is trustworthy. He has proven Himself faithful. But what a wonder that He trusts us. He put His plan in our hands and His Spirit in us. That alone should inspire us to act on our assignment.

Remember, the first man of God's creation, Adam, had been sanctioned while in the garden of Eden. In a daring act of impartation, God equipped Adam and Eve with a mandate: be fruitful, multiply, fill the earth, subdue, and have dominion.[49] And, having established that trust, He released them to their work. Certainly God knew the enemy was present and would seek out His creation, but God gave no warning to Adam about the question the serpent was about to ask Eve: *"Has God indeed said, 'You shall not eat of every tree of the garden'?"* [50]

God trusted Adam to do the right thing. But, standing alongside Eve, Adam does nothing to intercede as Eve takes the bait that put the hook in the mouths of all their descendants.

When we understand how critical each of us is to His plan, how could we continue a life in the city or at the gate?

Second, God has unfathomable love and compassion for those who have not yet found Him. We are well practiced in our creeds and traditions. We are sufficiently religious. For many, the clearest expression of faith takes place in a church building. That's beautiful. But what good is it? Other believers don't need us nearly as much as unbelievers do. Our churches are places of fellowship and teaching and instruction—and this is good—but Jesus didn't die only for the people we meet there. He died for everyone.

The extravagant price Jesus paid for each of us establishes that each of us has the same value. Even as we see those outside the church as lost or sinners or unbelievers, He sees us all as bought and paid for. He is the Good King who loves everyone who lives in His kingdom—even those who dispute His authority.

The real difference is that believers enter into an eternal relationship with the King after discovering what was done for them. I'm convinced that, once a person grasps this, he or she can't resist God's love that was, with grace, given. As Paul wrote in his letter to the church in Rome: *How, then, shall they call on Him in whom they have not believed? And how shall they believe in Him of whom they have not heard? And how shall they hear without a preacher?*[51]

Understanding Jesus' love and compassion for people can inspire us to express our faith outside of the city and away from the gate. Although no amount of activity could settle our account of sin, how we live matters.

Third, God's message is good news for a hurting world. The scribes and Pharisees brought the woman caught in adultery before Jesus. The law was clear. No mercy. She was guilty and, hence, condemned to be stoned.

The religious leaders hoped to take care of two bits of business: condemn Jesus with the Mosaic law and condemn the woman for her act. But Jesus turned the moment around when He pronounced, *"He who is without sin among you, let him throw a stone at her first."*[52]

Only one person was qualified to throw that stone—the One speaking. And He didn't. Instead, He reconciled her to God, abolishing the verdict.

Believers are called as ministers of reconciliation.[53] We connect people with God. That is our ministry. We can go outside the walls where the people are and become what may be the only representation of God they ever see and the only opportunity for their verdict to be annulled. For the accused and guilty, we have the good news of the gospel, and God's power is in the declaration of reconciliation for the condemned as we return with news of a treasure to be found.

What are your dreams in Him? Take this to Him in prayer, absent the restrictions of Fear.

Is there not a cause?

The gate is unlocked. And there is One who has gone before you. He has proven that He has vanquished every foe.

Section Two

FINDING THE CAUSE

And I heard the voice of the Lord, saying, "Whom shall I send? And who will go for Us?"

Then I said, "Here am I! Send me."

Isaiah 6:8

Chapter 4

UNLIKELY HEROES

"Necesito un barco." [54]

N No sooner had the words left my mouth than the driver gunned the engine, jumping the curb into oncoming traffic. Horns blasted and the seemingly never-ending line of halted vehicles to my right blurred past and confirmed I'd made the right call.

I did, in fact, need a boat.

Striking police officers closed the bridge that spanned the expansive Paraná River between Corrientes and Resistencia. And I needed to get to Resistencia. ASAP. *En seguida.* Right away.

I was serving as organizer for a conference opening that night, and I'd flown into town ahead of the rest of the team to oversee the setup of the conference site and to organize the volunteers provided by the churches.

Because Corrientes had the better airline schedule from Buenos Aires, it made sense to fly into their airport and take the quick drive over the river to the sister-city. But the line of police officers at the top of the bridge had a different idea.

We left the paved road and bounced through the back streets of Corrientes, Argentina, leaving the tourist district of casinos behind and careening past lean-to homes with barefoot children and mongrel dogs running around, kicking up the dirt.

We slid to a stop in a cloud of dust at a collection of riverside fishing shacks. Quickly, gasoline was brought in two-liter soda bottles and poured into the single-cylinder engine strapped to a primitive fishing boat.

I hopped into the vessel with a young man named Adriel who spoke with a beautiful accent. "When I woke up this morning," he said, "I had no idea that I'd be crossing the Paraná River with a representative of the great T. L. Osborn!" The two of us bang-clanked across the river and met up with a driver on the other side who rushed us to the city.

Perhaps it wasn't as critical as the saving of Samaria, but Adriel's availability and willingness to be used by God—on a day, for him, like any other—allowed the message of salvation to be boldly preached in Resistencia.

Adriel saved the day. God saved the city.

THE LEAST OF THE WEAKEST

God seems to enjoy surprising us with who—or what—He'll use.

Perhaps you're familiar with the verses found in Paul's first letter to the church in Corinth:

> *But God has chosen the foolish things of the world to put to shame the wise, and God has chosen the weak things of the world to put to shame the things which are mighty; and the base things of this world and the things which are despised God has chosen, and the things which are not, to bring to nothing the things that are, that no flesh should glory in His presence.* [55]

Life and Scripture are full of unlikely heroes. Our lepers sitting at the gate of Samaria are only a few.

But what's the message in all this? God desires to reveal to us that an ordinary person can carry an extraordinary purpose and the marvelous can be hidden in the mundane.

Now think about these two simple but not-so-easy-to-answer questions: Is there something exceptional waiting to break forth from an unlikely hero? And could that hero be you?

ANOTHER TIME, ANOTHER STORY

Sometime between 1100 and 1200 BC, God's people suffered under a siege slightly different from the one the Samarians faced. With frequent, plunderous raids, the Midianites, Amalekites, and others had a young Israeli man named Gideon and his fellow Israelites pinned up in the mountains.[56] God's people had been driven to dens, caves, and strongholds. Food was scarce. And so was courage.

Reeling from generations of on-again, off-again roller-coaster service and non-service to God, the Israelites cried out for deliverance. God heard their cry. First, He sent a prophet to the people, and then He sent the angel of the Lord to sit with Gideon—who'd been frightened enough by the Midianites to attempt to thresh wheat in a winepress—under an oak tree.

If Gideon feared the Midianites that much, we can only imagine how he felt when the angel greeted him with *"The Lord is with you, mighty man of valor."*

Kind of an odd moniker for a man who was hiding as he threshed wheat.

Gideon responded with a question: *"If the Lord is with us, why then has all this happened to us? And where are all His miracles which our fathers told us about, saying, 'Did not the Lord bring us up out of Egypt?' But now the Lord has forsaken us and delivered us into the hands of the Midianites."*

In reality, God hadn't done the leaving. But the angel didn't dwell on that. In true God-fashion, he said, *"Go in this might of yours, and you shall save Israel from the hand of the Midianites."*

We can only imagine Gideon's expression because the angel followed his command with *"Have I not sent you?"*

Gideon responded, *"O my Lord, how can I save Israel? Indeed my clan is the weakest in Manasseh, and I am the least in my father's house."*

This unlikely hero had every reason to reject the idea that he'd be used to bring victory to God's people. First, they didn't deserve it. God Himself had given them over to the Midianites to begin with because of their idolatry and worship of other gods. In Gideon's mind, deliverance probably seemed unlikely. In fact, it was far more likely that the angel would strike him dead for his lack of faith than use him to deliver Israel.

What would you say to the angel of the Lord if he stood before you right now, wherever you are—hiding in a winepress, sitting at your desk, or standing between the pews singing a hymn on a Sunday morning—and asked, "Have I not sent you?"

Gideon's "How can I...?" is probably not too far from what I'd say.

And then Gideon, unsure of his own identity, asked the angel to provide proof of who he was. (Many theologians believe this was an Old Testament Christophany—an appearance of Christ before the incarnation.)

But the Lord had a different plan. In spite of Gideon's questions and call for credentials, he, the least of the weakest, was chosen.

After a bout with doubt and a fleece or two to seal his faith,[57] Gideon, in a daring nighttime raid of his own, destroyed the tokens to the false gods and built an altar to the Lord. This cleared the way for the unlikely hero to deliver the victory the angel had promised. Soon thereafter, God gave Gideon—along with 300 soldiers who lapped the water of a spring like dogs[58]—victory over the Midianites.

But what does Gideon's story say about God's choice of heroes?

I won't digress into a dissertation on predestination or the sovereignty of God. Indeed, I am ill equipped theologically to hold you to any of my opinions on the subject, but scriptural evidence testifies that God will use whomever He chooses to use.

Gideon was far from the man of great faith and conviction that we, in the contemporary church, contend is necessary for victory. Because of that contention, we disqualify ourselves when we don't live up to an ideal. But pay attention: Gideon doubted. Gideon questioned. Gideon was far from ready for what God required of him.

But God still used Gideon.

A few years ago, I was asked by the founding board of directors of Trail Life USA (of which I was a member) to serve as its first chief operating officer while they searched for a CEO. I felt equipped for the work and had, for all intents and purposes, been serving in the role for several months voluntarily. Three months later, they called me in and asked me to serve as CEO.

And I thought, *How can I?*

I then spouted out a litany of Gideon-like excuses:

- "I've never been a Boy Scout."
- "I'm not much of a camper, I'm not known for my physical prowess, and I'm being called to lead an adventure organization for men and boys?"
- "But I've never led anything larger than a regional business and that for just a short period."
- "Lead? I'd much rather support a leader. God, what are you thinking?"
- "We've got one shot at this," I argued. "If Trail Life USA isn't successful," I told the Lord, "it's very unlikely that anyone will ever try this again. They will point to the time someone tried to start a Christ-centered, boy-focused outdoor organization and failed. That would be my legacy."

But, as God so gently reminded me, our doubts shouldn't define us. Nor should our accomplishments, for that matter. I'm sure we aren't capable, and I'm especially sure that I'm not.

That's the point.

The result in my case is that, for the first three years, I woke up in the middle of every night to wrestle with God and my insecurities. I hugged Him tighter. I knew I wasn't capable. And, in some God-typical way, it may have been that fact which qualified me.

Because I knew I couldn't, I had to lean on the One who could.

The experience led me to conclude that unless we're doing something beyond our own abilities—and leaning entirely on God—we may be wasting our time. If it's impossible to please God without faith, living a life that requires no faith is unlikely to please Him. Period.

"WHAT IS THAT IN YOUR HAND?"

Let's go further back. The year is somewhere around 1500 BC. The situation for the children of Israel was bleak. Over the course of 400 years of living in Egypt, God's people had prospered. But the new pharaoh didn't know or remember the Hebrew ruler named Joseph[59] who had brought the blessing of God to Egypt by his interpretation of dreams and his wise stewardship.[60] The current pharaoh was troubled—perhaps threatened—by the Israelites.

So he put taskmasters (chiefs of slave gangs) over them and made harsh demands regarding Hebrew newborns: midwives should kill males at birth. He did this, perhaps, to avoid the creation of an Israeli army. Despite this, the Israelites continued to flourish, so the pharaoh stepped up his oppression.

Moses was born into this environment. Although he should've been killed at birth, he experienced divine intervention when Pharaoh's daughter spared his life. Forty years later, reacting to the mistreatment of one of his Hebrew brethren, Moses killed an Egyptian, which became the first link in a chain of events that sent him hundreds of miles into the desert.

And that's where Moses first met God, forty years after he fled Egypt.

Far from the city, peacefully watching his sheep.

And then one day, at a burning bush, God challenged him to return to Egypt. To face his people and Pharaoh. To boldly walk back into a land where he was a wanted man and to demand that Pharaoh release the people of God.

Moses was understandably unsure. He answered God's command by saying, "*Suppose they will not believe me or listen to my voice; suppose they say, 'The Lord has not appeared to you'?*"

So the Lord said to him, "What is that in your hand?"

He said, "A rod."[61]

"What is that in your hand?" A simple enough question for a shepherd who probably always had his staff in his hand. It had become for him, perhaps, a natural extension of his body. It defined his call and equipped him to carry it out.

But God had greater plans. *"Cast it on the ground,"* He said. And the rod became a serpent.[62]

What do you have in your hand that has a greater purpose for the kingdom? What talent, extension, or ability can serve a greater purpose by being cast down than by being squeezed tightly in your fist?

On this side of the cross, we are God's choice. Imagine that. In spite of our questions and doubts and issues of self-worth, God has chosen us. We are His partners in the conquest of His creation for His glory. In the deliverance of His people from slavery. In the feeding of a besieged city. In the big kingdom business He has for you. That's why Paul could write these opening words in his letter to the church in Ephesus:

> *Blessed be the God and Father of our Lord Jesus Christ, who has blessed us with every spiritual blessing in the heavenly places in Christ, just as He chose us in Him before the foundation of the world that we should be holy and without blame before Him in love, having predestined us to adoption as sons by Jesus Christ to Himself, according to the good pleasure of His will, to the praise of the glory of His grace, by which He made us accepted in the Beloved.*[63]

The very things we think exclude us, sanction us for His service.

God loves the impossible. He lives in that realm. We limit ourselves to what we believe we can do while He calls us to do what we can't do.

When we look at all these unlikely heroes—the lepers, Gideon, Moses, and so many others—we see that their uncertainty, doubt, and weakness didn't invalidate them. One could argue that faith needs uncertainty, like an opposing bookend. Without uncertainty, faith isn't necessary, and *without faith it is impossible to please God.*[64]

ARE YOU TALKING TO ME?

I'm highly suspicious that when Jesus said, *"Go into all the world and preach the gospel to every creature,"*[65] He was talking to more than those who could physically hear Him. He was also talking to us. Or better yet, to me.

Exactly which part of *go* don't we understand? A thorough study of the original word reveals that it could be translated more accurately as "in your going." That means *going* is as much a part of us as our staff or some other instrument that defines us. We have what it takes to do what He invites us to do.

Sure, it may seem respectful, even acceptable, to live at the gate and applaud those who enter and exit. Way to go, Gideon! Nice work, Moses! You rock, Mother Teresa! But if we're called to great things, it's outright disobedience to do anything but respond to the call. "Attaboys!" don't cut it. Only flat-out, sold-out, all-in, and all-out obedience to the call cuts it.

No matter what form it comes in.

The gate offers a false sense of security that blankets the opportunity for true victory. It's a counterfeit life. There may be activity there. People come and go. We hear their stories and live vicariously and anonymously, clinging to our security and safety as the city starves and the Syrians celebrate.

Even the city, because of the ordinariness of existence and relative low expectations, can numb us to the greatness within us. We think that because we keep pace with those around us, we're keeping pace with the plan of God for our lives.

We couldn't be more wrong.

How can we be so indifferent? How can we not ask the question the lepers asked?

City or gate, God calls us to rise above the status quo, to look over the walls and beyond the gate to the victory that has been secured for us. When we take hold of the greatness and acknowledge the potential within us, we'll reject a mediocre life. We were built for something better than that. And our response to the call and question validates the price paid to secure us as partners with God in acquiring the treasure for the city.

We are the today-heroes of His story.

Shifting this responsibility to ministry leaders would be easy. But are others more qualified? In my experience with ministry leaders around the world, the ones we consider successful or anointed are the ones who simply stepped out and took a chance. They trusted that God trusted them. They left their city or gate and pursued a treasure sufficient to satisfy a city.

Their experience in finding God faithful produced a confidence that looks like what we have come to call "the anointing." They may have no special anointing. After all, the same Spirit lives in them who lives in you and me—the same Spirit Jesus had, the one who raised Him from the dead.[66] The Christ (the anointed One) in the body of the man called Jesus has become the Christ in you!

This is one of the great surprises (Paul called it a "mystery") of the gospel: *Christ in you, the hope of glory.*[67]

God's plan depends on you.

Not a select few.

Here's the terrifying thing to those of us resisting the charge to leave the gate: God let Moses pick up his staff again. But when he did, it changed. It became a God-rod.

When we let God have our talents and abilities, He supercharges them and makes us better than we were. Maybe not richer or safer or more secure, and certainly not more popular, but better. Better for the kingdom and more fit for His service.

That's where we truly live. Away from the gate and right in the middle of hugging Him tighter every moment, because every moment depends on His faithfulness.

Chapter 5

How Big Is Your God?

Years ago, self-respect was a common focus of our society. And then a new kid came to town. Self-esteem.

Look up *self-respect* in a dictionary, and you'll find several definitions, which all indicate that self-respect is something to be proud of. "A proper respect," Merriam-Webster says. "High or special regard: esteem."[68]

Respect is that act of regard we baby boomers were taught to give to those who were older than we were—in our family, in our church, in our parents' circle of friends, our teachers, our school principal, and so on. When that same regard is turned inward, we treat ourselves with dignity and decorum. We don't deliberately harm our body because it's the temple of the Holy Spirit.[69] We fill our minds—by what we read and what we watch—with good things. We understand the whole garbage in, garbage out concept. We respect ourselves.

And then there's self-esteem.

Dictionary.com defines this concept as "a realistic respect for or favorable impression of oneself; self-respect; an inordinately or exaggeratedly favorable impression of oneself."[70]

Self-respect and self-esteem are dependent on each other, and our impression of ourself is an important factor in recognizing what we are capable of doing or being. But how accurate can an impression of one's self be?

In the book of Jeremiah, we read that *the heart is deceitful above all things and desperately wicked; who can know it?*[71] In truth, our esteem isn't birthed within ourselves. It's a reflection or echo of what others see in us, what they say to or about us. To take it one step further, our self-esteem is clouded because it's what we think the most important people in our lives think about us.

As Jeremiah suggested, we're not accurate assessors of our own state. We need an outside perspective. And this perspective, good or bad, shapes the mirror we use to view ourselves. Furthermore, the way we view ourselves determines whether we'll starve in the city, wither at the gate, or launch upward and outward in search of the treasure.

I recently spent some time with a young man who felt he'd disappointed me. For a number of weeks, he'd walked in shame and guilt over a sin for which he had repented. But his sense of what he thought I thought about him affected his whole disposition. He said he felt as if the heavens were closed to him. His relationships with God, his friends, and his coworkers were tainted by the way he felt about himself, which had risen out of what he thought that I thought about him.

What relief he experienced when I confirmed my love and respect for him. In doing that, I also confirmed his heavenly Father's love for him. I watched his countenance change—from the shame that seemed to darken his appearance to a light that shone from within.

But who do you think affects the way we see ourselves the most? Those we are closest to or those we only know at an arm's length? You're right if you answered that the people nearest and dearest to us most affect the way we see ourselves. But the way we see ourselves also affects our behavior.

My high school days were nondescript until I reached my junior year. Then our band director/teacher expressed his belief in me. He saw qualities, strengths, and abilities in me I'd never seen in myself, and he honed in on those things, encouraging me to do the same. The way I saw myself changed. I went from wallflower to president or vice-president of almost every organization on campus in the course of a single year. The change in perspective and confidence as others saw me—different from my previous perspective—carried me through college, where I also became a campus leader.

What can account for such change? After my teacher spoke and worked with me, I then had an adjusted sense of my value and worth. I believed someone who, in my estimation, knew what I needed to know ... about myself.

We know where self-respect, self-esteem, and (inclusively) self-worth can come from. But where should they come from?

Through Jeremiah, God says, *"I, the Lord, search the heart, I test the mind, even to give every man according to his ways, according to the fruit of his doings."* [72]

Ab(normal) Use

Years ago, I updated the RAM in my laptop. I don't know where I found the courage, but I took off the bottom cover of my computer, yanked out a piece of plastic with a bunch of little blocky squares and dots on it, and replaced it with a piece of plastic that looked almost identical.

After that, things seem to work better.

I'd heard that people of normal intelligence can accomplish such things, and I frequently declare that what one man can do another man can do. I also figured that, since I'm a blogger, I should be able to remove the back of my laptop, if for no other reason than to see how my words get to the Internet.

If you'd walked up to me and handed me that piece of plastic, I would've been clueless about its purpose. Fortunately, I knew it was coming in the mail because I ordered it. If I hadn't been expecting it, I'm not sure what I would've done with it. It may have ended up under the leg of a shaky table or serving as a really cool bookmark. I would've or could've found a use for it. Something that, in the end, would've been abnormal use … or abuse. The disconnect with the creator's purpose would have yielded disappointing results.

Happily, the plastic piece ended up where it was created to function at its best. It's working right now, performing at its best and helping me to get these words to you. Humming along (if RAM hums) and doing what RAM does best.

You probably know where I'm going with this.

When we allow our creator to establish our esteem and worth—above what any ordinary person thinks—and to position us for our best use, we function at our best. If we misunderstand or underestimate what we are capable of or allow it to be determined by someone other than our creator, we accept an abnormal use rather than what He designed us to be and do. We may experience some moments of humming, but extended humming for our highest purpose will remain beyond our reach.

The Creator knows us best. This means He also knows what is best for us. Scripture says, *Surely you have things turned around! Shall the potter be esteemed as the clay; for shall the thing made say of him who made it, "He did not make me"? Or shall the thing formed say of him who formed it, "He has not understanding"?*[73]

When we partner with our creator in the grand adventure of the realization and pursuit of the treasure, we get closer to doing what we do best. Better still, the journey itself becomes worthwhile as we grow closer to the One who made us and knows us best.

The lepers sensed it. They knew that the day they left the gate—the day they found themselves in the middle of all that silver and gold and clothes—was a *day of good news.*[74]

Our decision to pursue God's purposes by escaping the city and letting go of the gate is the beginning of confirming our greatest use. The journey energizes our confidence, and this new confidence stimulates further exploits. No amount of affirmation from another person will come close to producing the self-esteem, self-worth, and self-respect of walking in what our creator planned for us.

The great psalmist King David wrote, *For You formed my inward parts; You covered me in my mother's womb.*[75] When we rightly think, "What does the most important Person in my life think about me?" our self-worth, self-respect, and self-esteem soar to heights that approach the heights set for us as God knit us together in our mother's womb! We fill the frame of the image we were shaped after.

Furthermore …

His will becomes our will.
His mind becomes our mind.
His compassion becomes our compassion.
His strength becomes our strength.
His priority becomes our priority.
His energy becomes our energy.
His anointing becomes our anointing.
His desire becomes our desire.
His peace becomes our peace.
His nature becomes our nature.
His status becomes our status.
His plan becomes our plan.
His destiny becomes our destiny.
His life becomes our life.
His purpose becomes our purpose.

Understanding and agreeing with what God thinks about us is the most critical element of Finding the Cause. When we partner with Him in what He thinks about us, we are on our way to encountering the treasure He has stored up for us. We grow in confidence, we realize our strength, and we are empowered with the passion to set out for the Syrian camp.

WHO AM I?

It's a question we all face at some point in life. More than simply being able to ask yourself the question, you must be able to answer the question.

But when you answer it, you should never answer as the world would. Nor should you answer in the way you, standing on your own, would. What you must do is answer the question as God would answer it about you.

But where does the answer come from? Where do we acquire such understanding?

From His Word.

Who am I?

- I am born again (John 1:12–13; 3:7; 1 Peter 1:23).
- I am saved (Acts 2:21; Ephesians 2:8; 2 Timothy 1:9; Titus 3:5).
- I am redeemed (Ephesians 1:7; Colossians 1:14; Hebrews 9:12; Revelation 5:9; 1 Peter 1:18–19).
- I am justified (Romans 5:1, 18; Galatians 3:24).
- I have a new nature (2 Corinthians 5:17; Galatians 6:15).
- Christ lives in me (2 Corinthians 6:16; John 14:23; Galatians 2:20; John 17:23; Colossians 1:27).

- I know He is my strength, my provider, my keeper (Philippians 4:13; Psalm 31:19; 2 Timothy 1:12; 2 Thessalonians 3:3; Jude 1:24).
- I know He is my partner, companion, and friend in life (Proverbs 18:24; John 15:13–16; 17:21–23).
- I am healed (Isaiah 53:4–5; 1 Peter 2:24; Exodus 15:26).
- I am provided for (Philippians 4:19; Psalm 84:11; 2 Corinthians 9:8).
- I am not afraid (Joshua 1:9; Psalm 27:1, 3; 23:4; 56:11; 91:1–7, 9–12; Isaiah 41:10).
- I am no longer condemned (Romans 8:1; John 5:24).
- I am delivered out of Satan's power (Colossians 1:12–14; Job 5:19; Daniel 6:27; 2 Corinthians 1:10).
- I am freed from the curse (Galatians 3:13).
- I am freed from captivity (John 8:32–36; Romans 6:22).
- I am connected to and complete in God (Ephesians 2:6; Colossians 2:9–10).
- I am free from my past defeat, and failure won't hold me back (Ephesians 2:1–7; 2 Corinthians 5:17).
- I am a partaker of the new nature (2 Peter 1:4; Colossians 1:12; Hebrews 3:14).

- I am a partaker of Christ's victory (Ephesians 2:5–6; Colossians 1:12–14).
- I have the righteousness of Jesus (Romans 5:17; Philippians 3:8–9; 1 Corinthians 1:30).
- I am more than a conqueror (Romans 8:37).

Have you ever watched a woodcrafter place a piece of wood into a lathe? By expertly rotating the drive and turning the wood, he can shape it to become the finished product he envisioned. Or have you ever seen a painter take a palette of paint and a blank canvas and—by expertly stroking the brush against the canvas—create a masterpiece?

Scripture reminds us that *we are God's workmanship, created in Christ Jesus for good works, which God prepared beforehand that we should walk in them.*[76] This is your confirmation that when God created you—as David said, "*in [your] mother's womb*"—He wasn't slapping paint onto a canvas, nor was He placing a piece of wood willy-nilly onto a lathe. You are His handiwork. He saw something in you long before you took your first breath. He had a unique plan and a purpose set aside for you.

Grab hold of that. God didn't prepare just anyone for your purpose.

God prepared you.

Chapter 6

WHO TOLD YOU THAT YOU WERE NAKED?

From the beginning, the fivefold God-given mandate has been to *be fruitful and multiply; fill the earth and subdue it; have dominion over the fish in the sea, over the birds of the air, and over every living thing that moves on the earth.*[77]

Assertive language that, in today's culture, seems threatening and presumptive. Almost dictatorial. Almost as if we shout to the fish, the birds, and other creatures, "If you don't do as we say or perform as we think you should, we'll squash you."

But truthfully, we human beings are, for the most part, nice folks who live decent lives rather than bold victors with a mission to reclaim the earth and its inhabitants under orders from the Creator-King.

Adam and Eve were given dominion over all God created, but in eating from the tree and questioning what they heard, they submitted to an entity other than their heavenly Father—an entity who had no interest in seeing them fulfill the mandate set by God.

The serpent's lie in the garden, in the form of a question, is the same lie he uses to deceive us: *"Has God indeed said …"*[78]

In the beginning days of Trail Life USA, an awkwardness in boldly proclaiming that we knew boys needed a Christ-centered, boy-focused outdoor adventure, character, and leadership experience hung between those of us who said it and many who heard it. This notion felt so countercultural in a world where voices proclaimed that gender is a social construct and has nothing to do with biology.

"Has God indeed said …?" became "Are you sure what you're proclaiming to be true is true? Is one-man-one-woman in marriage important? Are boys and girls so different that they require different programs to excel in their individual strengths?"

But brave men and women stood on principle and, in the process, a crowd gathered. The sound was made, and it rang true in the hearts of many. In less than three years, the organization grew to over 25,000 members, with over 700 churches on board.

At times we look back on the story of Adam and Eve with disdain. Or confusion. How could two people who'd been given so much and who'd walked with God in the cool of the evenings, how could that man and that woman have heard God incorrectly? How could the words from a creature they apparently saw only that one time discredit the truth they'd established with their creator and cast such a veil of confusion?

Surely we would never be that … stupid.

But think about it: how often does the atmosphere in which we live cloud our hearing and infiltrate the most basic truths we've heard from God?

The shame and the disorientation of our fallen selves cause us to find the nearest fig tree, pull some leaves, and sew them into cover-ups, as Adam and Eve did. And by doing so, our shame and disorientation inhibit our ability to be fruitful and to multiply, which was the first part of the mandate. Although we are created in the image of God, in our humiliation we submit to a low-life being that lacks the reproductive power and potential of our creator. Spiritual vertigo sets in and we spin … until Jesus comes into our lives.

It takes the sinless Son of God and Man to redeem us, restoring our glory, reestablishing our mandate, and setting our feet on the Solid Rock.

Jesus' words from the cross, *"It is finished,"* [79] and His words spoken to John from His throne, *"It is done,"* [80] declare the intent of God and counter the question the Enemy poses.

Yes. God indeed has said.

IN OUR SILENCE, GOD WILL SPEAK

Yet stepping out with bold proclamations requires balance. Speaking too much or deciding not to speak carry equal danger. I often find myself scrolling past rants on social media and tuning out talking heads on TV who repeat their party's lines.

Frankly, I'm overwhelmed by the number of words I encounter on a daily basis. And, even more frankly, I don't believe we were designed to handle so many messages at once. We used to say that people need to change the topic every twenty minutes to engage youth. Now—look at the numerous feed crawls and crammed screens of their phones and computers—you need multiple messages simultaneously to keep their interest.

We are deafened by the number of words we hear, each one clamoring for our attention. In the chaos, we must find the place for a word—or no words—*spoken in due season.*[81]

I've recently been more purposeful in getting quiet, in letting God speak, or, more accurately, hearing what He has already been saying. Years ago, part of my counseling training included sessions with a professor and an entire class behind a two-way mirror. One day I counseled a suicidal young man who acted out during the session. Instead of getting caught up in the outrage,

I prayed silently for the Holy Spirit to speak through me. I said nothing.

In the evaluation session that followed, the professor said, "There was a point where you were utterly calm, and the whole session took a different direction. Your client appeared to settle down without your intervention." The whole class seemed to lean forward as he asked, "What was going on in you at the moment?"

I took a deep breath and answered, "I was praying for God's help."

I was not attending a Christian university. Earlier in the semester (indeed, throughout my entire time in that graduate program), my faith was challenged by the professors and students. I felt I had to perform better than others because I had a stereotype to overcome. In that moment, however, God shined bright. He spoke through me.

Without a single word.

OUR EXAMPLE

Much of the time, we use words to create, correct, or restore our public image. It can be difficult to resist the temptation to defend ourselves, to explain ourselves, or to return a barb.

But in our silence, God will speak.

How much do we trust God? Will we let Him speak in the silence? Or will we fill it with our words?

Jesus showed us the way. Jerusalem was rife with drama as He was brought before the authorities. False accusations and lies were thrust at Him.

But, Matthew's gospel tells us, *Jesus kept silent.*[82]

Peter expands on this thought in his first letter by quoting Isaiah and saying, *"[Jesus] committed no sin, nor was deceit found in His mouth, who, when He was reviled, did not revile in return; when He suffered, He did not threaten, but committed Himself to Him who judges righteously."*[83]

The late Edwin Louis Cole—teacher and mentor to men—is quoted as saying, "Knowledge of God's Word is a bulwark against deception, temptation, accusation, even persecution."[84]

When accused or slandered, know what God says about you and believe it. In this way, He speaks in your silence. To you. And the voice of the Accuser is silenced.

Occasionally, you might even find elements of truth in the accusation. The Enemy, in his rush to condemn, can bring conviction that leads to godly repentance. The Holy Spirit is the Great Teacher and Counselor and will lead you into truth. With this in mind, when you're silent, allow the Holy Spirit to speak to your heart about what is true and to nullify what is false.

It's easy to cry out, "But what about what others think?"

Don't worry. God will take care of them.

The king and psalmist of Israel, David, penned these words: *Truly my soul silently waits for God; from Him comes my salvation. He only is my rock and my salvation; He is my defense; I shall not be greatly moved.*[85]

Christ was accused so we would not be condemned; if at any time we find ourselves accused, we cannot expect to manage with our words what He managed with His silence.

Enough said.

Chapter 7

THE RANSOMED BECAME A RANSOM

A potential danger in the type of living I'm propos-ing is that somehow, in wholeheartedly pursuing the implications of the core message of the gospel, we may forget the core message of the gospel.

In the work of walking out our call to a more abun-dant life, we must keep the atoning, completed work of Christ on the cross as the central focus of our lives. Even the critical aims of this book's message—being in the center of our calling, taking real risks for the Lord's work, being stewards of our talents—are as *filthy rags* apart from Christ's completed work.[86]

This is the crux of the matter. That He died for us. His righteousness makes us righteous.

RESISTING THE POPULAR GOSPEL

So how do we resist a popular gospel, which encour-ages success and self-fulfillment, without neglecting the call to pursue our fullness in Him? We commit ourselves to using Jesus' example by our commitment to be people who use His example of what it means to participate in kingdom living, His example of what success means in that endeavor.

Is it a revolutionary thought that the kind of life Jesus calls us to is the example He set? I was privileged to serve Dr. T. L. Osborn for a number of years. Without fear of being contradicted, I can say that in over fifty years of ministry in hundreds of countries and in dozens of published books, he never departed from speaking about our call to follow the example of Jesus.

There is great benefit in seeing this core truth as it brings salvation to the lost, sight to the blind, strength to the weak, dignity to the shamed, purpose to the wayward, hope to the hopeless, and light to those in darkness.

If we are going to follow Him faithfully, we must follow Him *as He was*.

As He Was

The earthly ministry of Jesus was growing. After standing before large crowds, teaching parables about sowers, lamps, and mustard seeds, Jesus told the disciples, *"Let us cross over to the other side,"*[87] meaning the other side of the Sea of Galilee.

Mark's next words are interesting: *Now when they had left the multitude, they took him along in the boat as he was.*[88]

Great confusion abounds in the church world over *how Jesus was*. In the 2,000 plus years since God was with us in Christ, religion, secularism, and political correctness have led to and contributed to our disorientation.

Don't be deceived. This is not a new strategy of the Enemy. It's straight from the garden of Eden. If the Enemy can get us to question what God has said, he will be successful at compromising truth within us. And compromised truth will produce a compromised victory.

Sure, the contemporary church seems to have success. We have vibrant music and meetings, great preaching and teaching. Beautiful buildings and TV shows and church programs. But do we take Jesus—or even take on Jesus—*as He was?*

It's hard to accept what we have now—this watered-down version of Christianity—as the life for which Jesus died so many years ago. Is this why God sent His only begotten Son? Was this the way He'd envisioned it … or even as the disciples experienced it when they moved out into the world and witnessed the growth of Christianity from the striking of a match to a flame? Let me be honest: when it comes to what we have in the church today, I may be willing to give my life, but would I give my son's life?

God may feel the same way. He envisions something more. And if we can, somehow, find our way back to the Truth—the *as-He-was* type of living—we'll be set free in the way He envisioned, which means we'll see the results He saw. To do this, we must do as the disciples did in Mark chapter 4 and take Jesus, *as He was*, to the other side.

"LET US"

Mark 4:35 begins with Jesus saying these two words: "Let us."

But why the *us* in this verse? Why did Jesus, the Son of God, need His disciples? Their influence? Their influence was nearly nonexistent. Their education? With the exception of one or two, they had little, if any, formal education. Their religious experience or training? To the contrary, His disciples were far from being students of organized religious thought. Advisors for His strategies? No. More often than not, He had to explain things to them, and even then they didn't quite grasp what He said. In fact, they rarely understood what He was up to until after He returned to heaven. And even then sometimes they missed the point entirely. Their financial support? No. They weren't wealthy ... and one was a thief. Emotional support? Not likely. In fact, in His hour of need, they slept.[89]

And yet these are among the most valuable skills and traits we'd seek in applicants if we had a plan to change the world.

88

Not Jesus. Jesus called common people. In fact, pick up your Bible and review the lives of those God called from Noah all the way to Paul and Barnabas, Timothy and Silas. The same pattern is repeated time and again.

But why? With all the qualified people in the world, why does He call those that many of us see as ill equipped?

Let's start with why He came at all.

A multitude of theological responses attempt to answer that question. Great men, wise men, who have pored over the Scriptures as a life's work have come up with answers—most of them somewhat convoluted and complicated. It may be as simple as this: God came because He needed to show us what we can be like.

"*Let us,*" Jesus said, because it was critical that those common people could see Him *as He was* to discover what (or who) they could become.

The word *us* is important because if the disciples (and we) can witness in His life what God wants to do in and through us, we can walk in the way we are called. Jesus calls us to follow Him so we can see what a man in relationship and partnership with God looks like and so we can see what the indwelling inspiration of the Holy Spirit looks like. Jesus came as our example.

The early church understood His reason for coming. He walked with them for three and a half years.

And they were called Christians because they did what He did—not just because they believed in Him. Luke references this when he begins the book of Acts with *the former account I made, O Theophilus, of all that Jesus began both to do and teach, until the day in which He was taken up, after He through the Holy Spirit had given commandments to the apostles whom He had chosen.*[90]

Began is the key word.

Beyond religious philosophy, empty ritual, fancy buildings, and spiritual organizations, the disciples did what Jesus began to do.

And so should we.

The Christ-life the disciples witnessed in Jesus was the example for their lives. And the Christ-life we witness through the Word and the Holy Spirit is an example for ours. Likewise, the Christ-life we live through the Holy Spirit is an example for us.

"Let us" is Jesus' invitation to observe His life so we can live ours in the same way. Not because of our riches or education or influence, but because of His example.

"CROSS OVER TO THE OTHER SIDE"

So, what should we do with what He has shown us through His example? We should follow His instructions: *"cross over to the other side."*

90

When Mark wrote those words he was referencing Jesus' desire to cross a lake (the Sea of Galilee) with the disciples. If we continue reading, we learn that along the way they encountered a storm. There's a great lesson in overcoming that storm, but it wasn't the reason for the trip. They crossed to the other side to free a demon-possessed man.[91]

But what about us? Why must we go over?

We must go over because people are unable to release themselves from their bonds, in whatever form that takes.

What is the *other side* for you? What thought pattern? What person? What neighbor? What coworker? What family member or family as a whole? What people? What nation?

Could it be that Jesus is calling you—like the lepers and the disciples in the boat were called—to take Him *as He was* and *cross over to the other side?*

The lepers set the city free. Jesus set the demoniac free. These are but two examples (of a countless number within the Bible's pages and within the annals of history) of God's ability to set someone free.

We know our creeds and traditions. We are faithful in our habits. But we forget that people in the church don't need us. Both the lepers and the religious folks of Jesus' day seemed content in their limited expressions of faith.

Jesus insisted on crossing the lake because people on the other side needed help. And because we have His example, we are the help. Being that help is vital to the continued existence of the church.

Paul asked these questions when he wrote to the church in Rome: *How then shall they call on Him whom they have not believed? And how shall they believe in Him of whom they have not heard? And how shall they hear without a preacher?*[92]

We are society-changers because we have Jesus' example to guide us and His Spirit within us. We are the creators and bringers of hope in a hopeless world. We are partners in His great plan of love that reaches the dying, the demon-possessed, and the lost.

We have good news! The power is in crossing to the other side, aware of who He was and who He is in us. With this knowledge and understanding, we can bring the good news.

We pray for Him to send His spirit or His angels to heal and touch people because we know that God is all-powerful and can heal from afar. But can't we be the angels sent to do what He told us to do? You see, He's not sending angels to the lost. He's sending us! He's telling us to cross over to the other side with the example of His faith, His life, His spirit, His virtue, His power, His goodness, His authority, His connection with God. It's in you, and it's in you right now. This very second.

A Certain Woman
and a Well at High Noon

Once you are called, and once you realize the Spirit living within you will give you the power to fulfill that call, no one said the crossing over will be problem-free. Jesus said that His burden is easy, and His yoke is light.[93] But to obtain that requires an all-in, *as-He-was* attitude.

There are often sacrifices to be made. Bridges to cross that seem rickety from the start. Places where it makes no sense for God to send anyone, let alone you. And yet, He did the same thing Himself.

It happened like this: Jesus and His disciples were returning to Galilee from the Judean countryside to deal with issues concerning John and baptism and who had baptized more than the other. On the way, Jesus stopped in Sychar—a town inhabited by the Samaritans, a Jewish mixed-breed from the Assyrian captivity.

The fully Jewish and the Samaritans weren't the best of cousins. In fact, the Jews of Jesus' day didn't speak or interact with the Samaritans unless absolutely necessary.

But Jesus knew that His calling involved more than getting back to Galilee. He had a divine appointment with a woman who lived in Sychar, one who—as an outcast—came to Jacob's Well to draw water at noon when the other women were long gone.

John's story of Jesus' encounter with the woman makes it clear that He knew exactly why He'd been called there. No, it didn't fit with the social mores of the era. In fact, the disciples were stunned and offended by the Teacher's behavior. But Jesus knew the woman at the well had a great need—and He had come to satisfy it. So much so, that when the disciples insisted Jesus eat something, He replied, "*My food is to do the will of Him who sent Me, and to finish His work.*"[94]

Even if it meant going into stinky ole Samaria.

Paul wrote,

I now rejoice in my sufferings for you, and fill up in my flesh what is lacking in the afflictions of Christ, for the sake of His body, which is the church, of which I became a minister according to the stewardship from God which was given to me for you, to fulfill the word of God, the mystery which has been from ages and from generations, but now has been revealed to His saints. To them God willed to make known what are the riches of the glory of this mystery among the Gentiles: which is Christ in you, the hope of glory.[95]

THE APPLICATION

If God can express Himself in the body of Jesus, and in the bodies of all those unfit for service we read about in the Old and New Testaments, then He can express Himself in your body. The stories of the Bible are the proof—and the resurrection of Jesus confirms—that the Spirit of God in a man or woman—*as He was*—changes that person forever. To choose God is to choose change. There is no escaping the fact that if you follow Him, He will remold you. It is challenging, tiring, painful, and inevitable.

But, glory to God.

The lepers of 2 Kings knew this. They embraced the reality of the riches in their hands and recognized the change that made them fit to be more than rejected disease carriers. Instead, they became carriers of great riches that would save the besieged. They gave up their selfishness and crossed over, as Jesus would have done, to make sure others were served. Their lives were ransomed. So they became a ransom for others.

Chapter 8

LEAVING YOUR COMFORT ZONE

To preface this chapter, allow me to make one thing clear: Everything I've spoken of so far, and everything I will speak of from here on, goes beyond your strength.

One has to wonder what the lepers were thinking when they decided to launch out. Their words were clear and their reasoning somewhat sound: *"Come, let us surrender to the army of the Syrians. If they keep us alive, we shall live; and if they kill us, we shall only die."* [96] But their proclamation is tinted with resignation and fatalism as well.

Each of us probably carries a bit of their attitude: we are somewhat restricted to a fate beyond our control; we aren't equipped for anything beyond what we can see. We seem to accentuate that train of thought in our Christian musings with one another: "If the Lord wills" or "I guess it was God's will." That's what makes it easy to stay on the couch. In our comfort zone.

What if the lepers—or Gideon or Jesus' disciples or the woman at the well—had simply accepted their

97

fate and attempted nothing? What if they'd taken inventory of themselves and determined they weren't up to the challenge? What if they decided that it was far easier to stay where they were?

Surely we depend on a sovereign God whose omnipresence, omnipotence, and omniscience are undeniable. But doesn't He continually call people to something greater than they could do on their own?

The lepers weren't reasoning about a plot to set the city free, even though that was the result of their action. As weak as they must've been, they left the gate and delivered a victory they couldn't have imagined. It surprised them, and they wrestled for a few moments with what they should do with what they received.

Our greatest victories in Jesus take place beyond our own abilities and expectations. They must. Our dependence on Him to sustain and use us beyond our weaknesses and away from the gate in ways that are beyond our expectations is exactly what qualifies us to be the kind of heroes who set cities (and lost souls) free.

As I previously stated, early in my service to Trail Life USA, I was keenly aware that I would be leaning heavily on God. I could point to hundreds of people more qualified, thousands more experienced. Nevertheless, God wasn't prompting them. He prompted me. Yes, I'm a father who wants the best for his boys. Yes, I understand the foundation on which the organization is built. Yes, I had some educational and professional experience that appeared to be beneficial. But surely, another person was more qualified. More experienced. Better suited.

Yet I had lived long enough to know that the person least qualified, but most aware of that fact, can be the person God is most likely to choose.

To leave your comfort zone and to encounter, on God's prompting, a challenge greater than you can handle may be exactly what He's calling you to do.

RUNNING ON EMPTY

Crammed into a Chevy Suburban fitted for bags of rice rather than our ragtag group—a youth pastor, a sidekick, a guide/driver, and four teens—we left the compound to head into the mountains to visit a village that likely hadn't seen outsiders in a generation or more. We bounced along the dirt road comically referred to as a highway, eventually leaving the road and steering toward a pass between two peaks across the hard-packed, dry sands.

Spirits were surprisingly high, even in the stifling heat of the enclosed truck bed. We laughed at cacti that seemed to strike poses as we passed. We sang every youth-group-bus-song we knew as we were jostled to the back of the truck bed when the terrain became steep and the nose of the truck pointed at the cloudless sky.

A look at my watch told me that in another ninety minutes we'd be through the pass. Hours and miles from civilization and, likely, any human beings besides the few families that inhabited the village on the other side of the pass, Juan, the guide/driver, began to argue. With himself.

I leaned across the bench seat that separated the bed from the front. "What's wrong?"

He stopped the truck and engaged the emergency brake to keep us from sliding backward. "*Casi vacío.*"

Almost empty.

Sure enough, the fuel gauge needle was all the way to the left. *Almost, Juan? More like totally.*

You find out what your group is really made of when you encounter a situation beyond your abilities. Our canteens were as empty as the gas tank, and the plan to refill them at the village evaporated. We knew the village had no vehicles and, hence, no gas.

Only one thing left to do.

We prayed.

Desperation refocuses and realigns. Although the gas mix-up was no fault of anyone in the vehicle, the only solution was dependence on Someone doing what we couldn't.

We watched, wide-eyed, as the needle crept up over the next few miles, eventually settling at just over a quarter tank—enough to get us home after our village visit.

I've seen a lot of miracles I can't explain. My natural mind, given enough time, tends to find a natural explanation for almost every wonder and phenomenon I've seen. Must have been a faulty gauge or the tilt of the vehicle, I determined months later.

But this I can't deny: God can do more with us through our dependence on Him in a tough spot than we can do if we depend solely on ourselves. It's not a call to test Him. We still have to do our part. But when He prompts, we must be willing to trust Him.

An Ever-brighter Path

The Bible says, *The path of the just is like the shining sun, that shines ever brighter unto the perfect day.*[97] As faulty human beings, we want to know what's coming before we let go of the gate. But the verse suggests that our path is fully revealed over time. We can have a sense of being in the right place and moving in the right direction, but it's not always clear.

Perhaps you've had that "Aha! That's what He's doing" experience when it all becomes clear. The challenge is the meantime—those periods of transition when the victory is somewhere up ahead and the gate is far behind us. That's the walk ... the path ... the life of faith.

But here's the caveat: we can't always wait for full daylight. We can't hold tight until all is clear. We must be willing to move when the path is beginning to brighten.

SEASONS OF TRANSITION

Life is full of transition.

Ed Cole wrote a book titled *Entering and Leaving Crisis: A Step by Step Guide for Times of Transition*. He noted we are constantly leaving one thing while entering another. He also made the point that the way we leave one thing will determine the way we enter the next.[98]

Christians may say we carry a "spirit" about us that may come from a recent experience or place. Or, regarding relationships, we may call them soul ties. In mental health circles, we refer to them as baggage or issues.

Either way, it's our personal responsibility and daily challenge to leave and enter appropriately, having resolved the experiences behind and having faith for the things ahead.

When handled in a godly manner, transition becomes the process whereby we capitalize on the events and experiences of the past, growing in godly wisdom and arriving at the next thing free of the disappointments and full of faith for the greater assignment.

In my experience, every event from my past, when handled and processed in God's grace and my hope in Him, is preparation for the next. Processing the past, walking in grace, resting in hope. That's God and me, in this together.

Partnership with God in His plan for creation requires that we grow and don't shrink back, that we hope and don't despair, and that we advance and don't retreat.

Transition carries a certain amount of anxiety, but, whether chosen or thrust upon us, our seasons of transition don't surprise God. He doesn't wake up one morning, see the changes, and say, "Well, I didn't see that one coming." Instead, He is fully in control of the outcome.

When we surrender to God, our life is His, which means that change is gonna come. It's inevitable. While we may be the agents of that change, He'll use our transitions to make sure we have the proper elements in our lives so the Christ-life can be formed in us.

The uncertain feeling that accompanies transition can point to areas in which we need to trust Him more. Areas where we're forced to remember that God sees the end from the beginning. Greater than the Wizard of Oz, He stands behind the curtain that hangs between us and the next scene of the drama that is our life. He is both in our present and in our future, going ahead to prepare a place for us. Truly, *all things work together for good to those who love God, to those who are the called according to His purpose.*[99]

Whether you initiated the transition or it is the result of circumstances beyond your control, God is never surprised by a millisecond or a microcosmic element of it.

Trust Him in it all, with it all, through it all.

MAKE READY A PEOPLE

A pastor in South America recently shared with me how his city experienced a great revival in the 1980s. The story goes that every one of the 40,000 inhabitants was saved through the efforts of an evangelist who ministered for several weeks in an outdoor campaign. The churches were packed to overflowing. The pastors were taxed to their limits as they handled the harvest of souls.

The tragedy is that, within a few months, church attendance was back to its pre-revival numbers.

"What happened?" I asked.

"There weren't enough churches to hold them" was his answer.

There is great truth here. There are not enough churches in the world for the harvest God has in mind. But there are enough believers being called by Him, called to step out and position themselves before the harvest is fully here.

Section Three

TAMING THE POWER OF INFLUENCE

Then [the lepers] said to one another, "We are not doing right. This day is a day of good news, and we remain silent. If we wait until morning light, some punishment will come upon us. Now therefore, come, let us go and tell the king's household."

2 Kings 7:9

Chapter 9

WE CAN'T KEEP THIS TO OURSELVES

The lepers stumbled on more than one treasure. They also encountered a principle that should drive every believer to live a life so countercultural in its unselfishness that God's graciousness cannot be denied.

Jesus' command to *go into all the world* with the good news of the gospel rather than keep it to ourselves is at the core of the building of His family. It wasn't merely a suggestion of what to do once He returned to heaven. The command was of vital importance. To Him. To the ancient world. To the world to come.

To us.

Jesus spent more than three years teaching and preparing His disciples to take not only what they'd seen and heard to the world but also what they'd experienced at the core of their being. They'd spent this training time in a tiny circle of friends, traveling within a tiny circle of the earth's surface. But He needed them to expand their borders and influence.

And they did.

History and tradition tell us that Andrew and John went to Greece, Thomas went east to India, Matthew and Philip went to Africa, Simon the Zealot went up and over to England, Thaddaeus went to Turkey, Peter went to Italy, and Bartholomew traveled to several countries—each of them carrying the good news of Jesus Christ, shouting and proclaiming and preaching what they knew to be true.

That which was from the beginning, John wrote in what is known as the First Epistle of John. He continued this way:

> *[That] which we have heard, which we have seen with our eyes, which we have looked upon, and our hands have handled, concerning the Word of life—the life was manifested, and we have seen, and bear witness, and declare to you that eternal life which was with the Father and was manifested to us—that which we have seen and heard we declare to you, that you also may have fellowship with us; and truly our fellowship is with the Father and with His Son Jesus Christ. And these things we write to you that your joy may be full.*[100]

As Dr. Steve Brown of Key Life Network said in a sermon, "When you've seen a dead man walking, you can't keep quiet."[101]

But more than that, when you've experienced walking with God on a day-to-day basis, when you've seen His miracles, felt His love, had your feet washed by the Master ... how can you *not* tell? How can you possibly stay home on the couch, even if it means traveling a long, long way to testify of what you've seen? Even if it means risking your life.

Like the disciples, when we discover what Jesus has done for us and the treasure that has been delivered, we should be compelled to tell others. But that isn't any more of a natural tendency for us than it was for the lepers. We are, at our worst and in our most natural state, selfish. We must be intentional about our decision to share the treasure, and we must be actively passing that passion to others.

SEE THE PEOPLE?

My family accompanied me as I coordinated a number of conferences and mass outreaches around the world. On one trip to the Caribbean, I made sure that Luke, who was eight years old at that time, had a chance to stand with me on the platform before the meeting started so he could see tens of thousands of faces waiting to hear the good news. "Can you see all those people?" I asked. "They are hungry for the gospel."

For a few moments, he scanned the crowd to take it all in. "Yes, Dad," he said. "I see."

We'd built up to that moment for some time. Our young sons were constantly reminded by "our little corner of the world"—a display of art that depicted the world's children in a corner of our kitchen—and the importance of being aware of the masses who need the treasure we'd stumbled on, the experiences we'd had with Jesus Christ. What our eyes had seen and our ears had heard. What we'd touched and been touched by.

For Luke, the Caribbean experience was flesh-and-blood reality of something he'd seen in his home and seen in the coming and going of his father to places beyond. But he needed to see it for himself. And so he did.

God does that for us. If He can show us the field, *white for harvest*, He can inspire us to share.[102] We'll be unable to slouch on the couch—or sit at the gate—another minute. We'll be like Jairus, whose daughter Jesus brought back to life, or the woman at the well, or any of the countless others Jesus touched, those whose lives He changed in unmatchable ways. We'll have to tell somebody.

Or tens of thousands of somebodies.

I'm fully convinced that when Jesus said, *"Go therefore and make disciples of all the nations,"* He meant it.[103] He meant it for those who heard Him speak those words. And He meant it for us.

What will you do with the treasure you've stumbled upon? Imagine the change the lepers experienced.

Maybe you'll go to other nations. I've taken dozens of people to the mission field and discovered that, although you go to change a nation, it's the nation that changes you.

Maybe you'll visit a neighbor, or the sick, or the captive. Maybe you'll extend yourself in a new way. One woman I know shops at stores that sell quality merchandise at a discount. Her ministry is to walk the aisles, waiting on a prompt to buy a particular item. Then she'll pray about who needs it. The testimonies of single moms who didn't have an outfit for that day's interview or didn't have the proper outfit to begin a new job are amazing.

Often, God will lead you to minister to those whose stories reflect something in your life. I've heard of women who, brought out of the muck and mire of strip clubs, make a 180-degree turn and take the gospel right back into the clubs. When they go, they take the dancers items they know they need along with the offer to buy them a cup of coffee or a meal. Once they sit at the table, they share their stories and help the girls—many who are trapped in this lifestyle—out of it.

We often hear of the homeless and drug-addicted who've been released from their chains by the power of Christ and His saving love, then go back to the streets to minister. Or of those released from incarceration who, once God has properly prepared them, take the gospel message to the very place that, at one time, held them captive.

But it doesn't have to be that drastic. Sometimes having an inexpressible love for children will lead a man or a woman to work within the judicial system, to become a foster parent, or to start a sidewalk Sunday school for children who may not enter through the double doors of a church. Sometimes missing a meal and going hungry for an hour or so will stir something deep inside that says, "There are dozens of hungry people in your own backyard, so why don't you join a ministry that feeds them?" And if there is no ministry, "why don't you start one?"

This is one of the truest definitions of ministry: to be delivered from something and then to live transparently enough to walk others out of that same bondage.

Still, sometimes God calls you to far-off places. For reasons you can't explain, you'll gladly sell all your worldly goods and join a team of missionaries.

Or perhaps, like me, you'll hear of a boys' organization that needs a leader.

How then will you share what you have?

I love this quote from Charles Spurgeon: "If the only result of our religion is the comfort of our poor little souls, if the beginning and the end of piety is contained within one's self, why, it is a strange thing to be in connection with the unselfish Jesus, and to be the fruit of his gracious Spirit. Surely, Jesus did not come to save us that we might live unto ourselves. He came to save us from selfishness."[104]

Indeed, it is a strange thing for our selfish souls to be connected to an unselfish Jesus. And a marvelous thing. A wonderful thing.

It forces us away from the gate. It shouts into the marrow of our souls and asks, "Why are you sitting here until you die?"

Chapter 10

TAKE INVENTORY

Put yourself in the lepers' shoes. Theirs was a dire situation, which means yours is too. If you go into the city, you die. If you stay at the gate, you die. Not many options remain. So what would you do?

Staying at the gate made no sense. But then again, neither did going. So, they chose what seemed the better option. They had no way of knowing their decision would have generational significance. In that one decision, they preserved the future of God's people—certainly the future of Samaria.

Anyone other than God would have dismissed them. With all the able-bodied men, capable of so much more than the four lepers, how could they be the answer to the city's desperate situation? Line up every man in Samaria and the fields surrounding in order of their likeliness to deliver the city, and these guys would be near the end of the line.

Yet, in all their weakness, the lepers had something essential: the ability to take inventory of their lives.

Look again at the story of Moses. For forty years, he walked alongside and behind sheep, coaxing them with a shepherd's crook-necked staff—the tool of his trade. And then, on a day that began like any other—but which proved to be like no other—he breathed in the smoke of a burning bush that boomed with God's voice. A voice that told him to return to Egypt and demand that Pharaoh *"let My people go."* [105]

Moses had legitimate excuses for not obeying. For staying at the gate. But God met every single one with logic and reason:

"Who am I that I should go to Pharaoh …"

"I will be with you …" (In other words, this isn't about you, Moses. This is about me.)

"Suppose I go to the Israelites and say to them, 'The God of your fathers has sent me to you,' and they ask me, "What is his name?"'

"This is what you are to say to the Israelites: "I AM has sent me to you."

"What if they do not believe me or listen to me and say, 'The Lord did not appear to you'?"

"What is that in your hand?"

"A staff." [106]

God told Moses to take inventory. But Moses had more than just the tool of his trade; he had palatial experience. He understood Egyptian laws and protocol. He was an inside-outsider: at one time in the inner circle and at another time cast out. With all arguments out of the way, Moses took that staff (after it became a snake and then a staff again) and returned to Egypt to do what God required: set the Hebrews free, something that would have generational significance.

Many times we hand our self-evaluation to others. We lean on their assessment rather than our own. Although it is important to have counsel, accountability, and helpful feedback from those near to us and those who may have helpful wisdom or experience, a fearless assessment of our inventory can't be completely outsourced.

What are your strengths? What are your passions? What are the clear promptings of your heart placed there by God to guide you in fulfilling your call? What is that in your hand?

Commit to a time or—better yet—a life of prayer and reflection that allows God to clarify for you what you have in your desert or your Samaria and at your burning bush or at your gate.

Moses had a talking bush. The lepers had one another. So then, like Moses who spent time talking with God about the situation and the lepers who voiced the question to one another at the gate, submit your concerns to those who can help refine and mirror for you what you see yourself.

Then lead with your strengths. The lepers may have been social outcasts, but they could still think. And they could walk. It wasn't much, but it was enough. Moses may have struggled with speaking to Pharaoh, but his brother Aaron was on his way to meet him midway in the desert, and Moses had the God of Israel with him. Had the lepers or Moses focused on their weaknesses, they may not have moved at all. The lepers would've stayed at the gate; Moses would've remained with his sheep. And the Samarians and the Hebrews would've been sunk.

We can get stuck if we focus on our weaknesses.

While a boy, I visited a dive shop in the Florida Keys, preparing to head out and do some scuba diving. My father struck up a conversation with another customer. Eventually the man asked, "Are you really going out there into that water? Aren't there sharks out there?"

It was a rather unremarkable conversation as conversations go, so why can I still recall it over forty years later? Because the man told us his name: Frank Borman. We recognized it, of course, because he was an astronaut. More specifically, one of the first three astronauts to circle the moon.

Commander Borman lived with an intense fear of being underwater with sharks, but he still strapped into a capsule on a rocket and circled the moon— something no one had done before. Something I dare say most beach-loving scuba divers would never even fathom doing.

But what if Borman's evaluation had stopped at the fear? What if his evaluation hadn't included the extraordinary strengths it took to endure such a journey?

What if Moses had gone no further than the bush and no farther than the desert? What if the lepers stopped at "leper"?

Where does your self-inventory stop?

DON'T STOP THERE

Once you've collected the data for your fearless assessment, determine how it can be enhanced. Educate yourself. Read. Develop. Ask questions.

Early in our marriage, my wife and I served as therapeutic foster parents in a newly developed program. Along with the broken boys came a dedicated therapist to help us through tough times and issues. We hung on every word and piece of advice of that first therapist—who also who wrote the program.

But then she left.

We could've quit. Without her, it was easy to see we didn't have what it took to bring the level of expertise or experience these boys needed. Like the lepers and Moses, our inventory was severely lacking. But we had our staff; we had our legs and our brains. We had something—we liked to learn. And a desire to learn set us on a course that eventually led to two master's degrees in Mental Health Counseling and Counseling Psychology.

We thought God enabled us to earn those degrees so we could help those broken boys. But the credentials also became part of the inventory He continued to draw on over the years as He used us in youth ministry, college and career ministry, premarital counseling, and young marrieds. Now those credentials help us to understand what boys need and to integrate that into the work of Trail Life USA.

God takes a shepherd and delivers *six hundred thousand men on foot, besides children.*[107] He takes four lepers and delivers a nation. He takes a clueless couple and uses them to encourage others. Each of those deliverances (and this is humbling to admit) leads to generational results.

In this same way, God can take what you have in your inventory or add to it and turn it into something greater than you can do on your own.

Remarkably, the experience you gain along the way also becomes part of your inventory. Dr. Osborn shared a story of two men who traveled from Africa to his home in Oklahoma. They knocked on his door and explained their desire. "Dr. Osborn," they said, "lay your hands on us and impart the anointing that has enabled you to impact so many around the world." Then they added, "And do it quickly, as we must get back to the airport to return to our homes in Africa."

Of course, he understood their hearts and passion for helping the lost. But he also understood that it was largely his experience, not any particular anointing alone, which made him successful in seeing changed lives. Decades in the field in dozens of countries had built an inventory of successes and failures that had prepared him. What appeared to an observer as an uncommon sensitivity to a specific event was actually the skillful application of a lesson learned—the use of a tool acquired along the way.

As we commit ourselves to allow God to use us at the edges of our own capabilities, we add to our inventory. Successes and failures, open and closed doors, leanings and learnings, and eyewitness experiences further equip us for His service as we expand to fill the space He designed for us.

Could this be what Jesus talked about in the parable of the talents?

For the kingdom of heaven is like a man traveling to a far country, who called his own servants and delivered his goods to them. And to one he gave five talents, to another two, and to another one, to each according to his own ability; and immediately he went on a journey. Then he who had received the five talents went and traded with them, and made another five talents. And likewise he who had received two gained two more also. But he who had received one went and dug in the ground, and hid his lord's money.[108]

The parable goes on to say that after a long time passed, the master returned to discover that the first two men had taken what was in their hand and put it to work, doubling the master's wealth. But the last man (who had gold in his hands just as the other two did) had done nothing with it.

And the master was not happy.

What was Jesus saying with this parable? The Master has given you all you need—some a little, some a lot—for that which He has called you to do.

"Do something with what He's given you," I say. "Grow your inventory."

The danger is in allowing what God has given you to produce arrogance or self-sufficiency. Remember, you live for an audience of One. He is the One who both calls you and equips you for what lies ahead.

Chapter 11

REAL INFLUENCE

I travel around the country and speak to groups of men about issues such as fatherlessness, boys in crisis, and essential skills for executives. These heart issues tend to open men up to vulnerability.

But it's risky.

Many times, while I'm talking with someone after a speech, one or two men will orbit me. Out of the corner of my eye, I recognize their struggle between mind and heart. It's a gate moment, in many cases, as the orbiter wrestles with the questions such as "Am I safe?" or "Can I trust?" He wants to leave the gate, but the security there—even if it's confining and starving him emotionally—is the devil he knows.

Sometimes I have to reach out and ask the opening question. Like a game of catch, somebody has to throw the ball first.

Me: "You look like you're struggling with something."

The Orbiter: "Me? No. I'm just thinking."

(Note to the reader: Guys don't struggle openly on their first toss. It's like trying some behind-the-back blind toss or a free throw from half-court when you first handle the ball. That level of vulnerability will come later.)

Me: "Me too." Sometimes when I hear myself say things, I wonder if I'm as authentic (or daring or caring) as I'm calling other men to be.

I needed to be vulnerable first. Real influence initiates. It doesn't only ask the question internally. It also stands up to leave the gate and engage whatever enemy confines it. The bottom line is that we can be lulled into complacency at the gate, or we can be prompted to step out and engage people, setting them free.

Recently I had an appointment with my eye doctor. This particular practice has a very engaged, verbal doctor. The nurses try to keep everybody moving through the appointment process because the doctor chooses to engage everybody, which means a patient can wait for hours beyond their appointment time.

To offset the patients' extended wait time, the staff developed a series of small waiting rooms through which you advance. It's like those theme park lines that take you through a series of doorways so you sense progress.

After I'd spent some time in the first waiting area, I was ushered into a room of about twelve people who'd clearly been there awhile. I engaged. "How's everybody doing?" I asked, sitting.

They glanced up from their phones to see who this crazy guy was. The ice was broken. The ball had been tossed. Thank goodness they wanted to play catch.

During the next half hour, we bonded as a group. Diverse as can be, names were exchanged, diagnoses compared. We debated the best coffee in town and the best offers for seniors. Elderly patients introduced their accompanying sons or daughters, and they gushed over each other openly: "She's always there for me." "She never complains." "He makes sure I get to the grocery store every week." On and on.

We scooted to the edge of our seats when the nurse came in and cheered whoever was called. "Keep in touch. Good luck. Nice talking with you."

Okay, I'll admit it. I snuck in a few gospel truths too.

Before leaving the room, one woman spoke for us all: "Usually I sit here and nobody talks. Today I feel like I spent the morning with friends."

It wasn't a cultural upheaval or the freeing of a city, but I'd like to think that when I initiated the conversation, everyone's lives were enriched and improved. All of them probably went home and shared about their new friends at the eye doctor. Some of them may be looking forward to their next appointment. I hope that one of them initiates the conversation next time. It's a minor victory, but it's an experience outside the city and away from the gate. In our daily walk, we can make a living or make a difference.

Influence takes a chance. It talks first, opens up first, sets the tone for the extraordinary. And it's in the extraordinary that captives are freed.

Remember when Jesus called His disciples to get into the boat? "*Let us cross over to the other side*," He said.[109]

Immediately they encountered a storm, but He calmed it, and they made it to the other side where He set the captive free.

Look at the words of Jesus again with me:

Let us. We must choose to join Him in the boat.

Cross over. It will take effort to get from Point A to Point B. Storms and difficulties will challenge our willingness to be used to influence another person.

To the other side. If we join Jesus and trust Him to calm the storm, we'll find solid ground and be positioned to set captives free.

When we understand that Jesus is always calling us to an "us" experience, initiating becomes easier. The expected storm is His responsibility, which means it isn't ours.

Here's the truth: You can't change a heart without engaging it. In a Christian culture that seems to value megachurches, TV churches, or online fellowship, we have to work extra hard to connect. To step out. To *cross over to the other side.* Face-to-face, eyeball-to-eye-ball. Full engagement utilizes a listening ear and a prompting heart that throws the first ball.

Homeschooling my boys was one of my favorite chapters of life. Freedom over my schedule let me arrange for visits from college kids during our academic downtime. Sometimes they spent an hour or two on my back porch sharing what was going on in their lives. Real influence happened. Beyond 140 characters and emojis, selfies, and private chats, connections were made and hearts were changed as words and time were shared.

Salvation happened there. Repentance happened there. Deliverance, awareness, and convictions happened there. Face-to-face because influence initiates.

Put yourself out there. And remember, you're not alone.

Chapter 12

WRITE THE VISION

Daily interactions can be enhanced and can lead to captives being set free. We can also set the table for the extraordinary hidden in the ordinary. But beyond these is the intentional pursuit of something that takes forethought, planning, and a commitment beyond the present.

How do we identify these opportunities for big kingdom business? How do we launch the boat, leave the gate, or throw the first ball? What does the call even look like?

For most of us, it's not an issue of trying to find what we should do but discerning what we're supposed to do. If we spend time exploring how others have engaged the core question and left the gate, we can be inspired by their stories and tempted to duplicate them. That's not a bad approach. It's certainly better than sitting at the gate or starving in the city. But what about a specific call that uses our individual design, unique experiences and talents, and available resources, all overlaid to point us to our calling? It's more of a revelation than a study. It's an intentional uncovering of the secret things hidden (by God, I believe) in our personalities and experiences that direct us to our calling.

Looking back is easier. We see how our past prepared us for our present. But how can we capture our past and our present to prepare us for what God's calling us to do in our future?

I like the counsel God gave Habakkuk: "*Write the vision and make it plain on tablets, that he may run who reads it.*"[110]

How do we, today, *write the vision*? Here's a practical way:

Consider a number of screens such as strainers or webs. If you stacked them one on top of another, you'd see how the holes closed up. If you stacked enough, there'd be fewer and fewer ways for something to pass through them. What if we used this analogy to intentionally write our revelation?

Maybe it's not precise, but it's helpful. It leaves our future much less to chance while positioning us to seek out God's leading as we consider what's possible.

Start with a column labeled Passions. When was the last time you were touched deeply by something? Was it in a movie? A book? An encounter of some sort? Write down the elements of those moments in that column. Then include what you love to do—what you'd choose to do if you had a free day or a free week.

If you looked at my Passions column, you'd see that I'd written "young people" and "travel." The testimony of a young person always touches me. And travel inspires me.

Your second column is Talents. What are you good at? Remember the woman who was so good at shopping and bargain hunting? She would list that in the Talents column. Combined with her passion for the needy, she turned it into a ministry.

Next is Resources. Remember when God asked Moses, *"What is that in your hand?"* [111] Now it's your turn to answer. What do you have readily available that could indicate a call? God always provides what we need to accomplish what He has called us to do. What do you have? Time? Money? A large home? A collection of trains? Think outside the box and fill the column with your resources.

Next is the column labeled Cultural Need or Relevant Applications. God will always have enough ideas for people who are willing to carry them out, and the world will always offer opportunity for Him to show Himself faithful through you. What does your community, the world, or your family need? Where would God put you to work?

If you get stuck as you fill in this column, keep this Scripture in mind: *The Lord is near to those who have a broken heart and saves such as have a contrite spirit.* [112] If you want to be where He is, find the brokenhearted and crushed in spirit. Those are the culturally needy you want to list.

You can add more columns if you want, such as What My Spouse Thinks I'm Good At or Geographic Interests.

Now draw lines across the columns that might connect entries. See if the vision becomes plain to you. The lepers' grid, if they pared it down to possibilities, would've looked something like this:

Passion	Talent	Resources	Cultural Need
To live	I can walk	A question	Starving city

My table for Trail Life USA may pare down to something like this:

Passion	Talent	Resources	Cultural Need
Young people	Creativity	**Time**	The lost
Travel	Music	**Education**	Orphans
Writing	**Organizational skills**	**Business experience**	Hope
Inspiring people		**Supportive family**	**Christ-centered, boy-focused outdoor adventure**

I can see clearly how the boldface entries lined up to make Trail Life a discernable vision.

Here's a blank table you can use:

Passion	Talent	Resources	Cultural Need

Now that the vision's plain, how will you run with it?

When I left the gate to help minister in other continents, my wife and I made the vision plain to our sons. We made it clear. We made it easy to understand. My grid for the work I did around the world would've looked something like this:

Passion	Talent	Resources	Cultural Need
Young people	Creativity	**Time**	**The lost**
Travel	Music	Education	Orphans
Writing	**Organizational skills**	**Business experience**	Hope
Inspiring people		**Supportive family**	Christ-centered, boy-focused outdoor adventure

When I launch a business, one of the first things I do is print a business card. In one of my earliest ventures, I ran an ad in the newspaper selling products I didn't own. Yet. My wife looked up from the cards and pointed out, "You don't have a business that does that."

"Yes I do, honey. See my business card?"

We laughed together, and it ended up being a very prosperous venture.

A few years later, when I declared I'd write, she decorated my office with the degrees and certifications that qualified me to write about the topic I had chosen. She made the vision plain and created an atmosphere that gave me the confidence to leave the gate.

Write your vision. Build your grid. See if it points you to the treasure so you can set people free.

THE TREASURE AWAITS YOU

Now the angel who talked with me came back and wakened me, as a man who is wakened out of his sleep. And he said to me, "What do you see?" So I said, "I am looking, and there is a lampstand of solid gold with a bowl on top of it, and on the stand seven lamps with seven pipes to the seven lamps. Two olive trees are by it, one at the right of the bowl and the other at its left." So I answered and spoke to the angel who talked with me, saying, "What are these, my Lord?" Then the angel who talked with me answered and said to me, "Do you not know what these are?" And I said, "No, my lord." So he answered and said to me: "This is the word of the Lord to Zerrubabel: "Not by might nor by power, but by My Spirit," says the Lord of hosts." Zechariah 4:1–6

Early readers of this manuscript cautioned against the thin line between the awareness and pursuit of a calling and humanism as the force that can lead one forward without any element of the divine.

It's true that we can do things on our own, without divine leading. Indeed, it's possible to live our entire lives faith-free and achieve what many call success. Each person reading this book—underlining its pages to highlight the words and phrases that mean the most to him or her—can name at least five to ten human beings currently living who are successful and yet have no (obvious) relationship with God. At least, not in the manner for which Christ died.

So how do we distinguish between a good idea and a godly calling? How would a leper know if it's time to stand and leave the gate because rational thought led him to do so rather than because the Holy Spirit prompted Him to launch out and set a city free?

That is, perhaps, the greatest challenge of pursuing wholeheartedly the fulfillment of your calling. The pursuit isn't for the faint of heart, so we can easily err on the side of doing things in our own strength. We can neglect the gentle nudge or still small voice that would lead us along a divine path and, based on our intelligence or experience, choose our own path instead.

That is a grave danger.

In the strongest of words, I counsel you to stay close to the One who should guide you. That closeness is essential in hearing His voice, not that of a stranger. The hourly dependence on Him and His leading, along with a careful understanding of His Word, is the greatest defense against missing the treasure.

Neither worldly success nor worldly failure is an indicator of one's place in the will of God. That measurement is beyond us. Indeed, sometimes what looks like failure is a deep work in the life of a man or woman clinging tightly to God, while what looks like success is a distraction.

But that doesn't mean we can or should fear success. Hidden in it, if our hearts are right, may be the divine will for our lives and the divine deliverance of a city.

Hug God tightly and ask yourself, "What has He put in my heart to do? What did the Creator intend for me?"

Then launch out.

Go. Cast the net on the other side. Cross over. Lift up your eyes. Write the vision. Take the course.

And live the unique story He wrote for you.

Four Guidelines for Vision Casting

1. Put your feet on the ground.

There was a time in our lives when we felt called to China. Was it God's call, or was it only an interest in extraordinary living and a chance to follow friends who'd chosen that path?

At the same time, I'd been asked to assist with a campaign in Japan. We interpreted that as a direction God was giving to that area of the world. But it wasn't enough direction. I took a flight from Japan to China and put my feet on the ground to weigh the fidelity of the call. Within twenty-four hours, I knew China was not for me. That was a bit shocking for a guy who has spent considerable time traveling—loving every minute—but I couldn't wait to get out of China. Why? Not because others, such as my friends, weren't supposed to be there, but because I wasn't supposed to be there. So strong was the conviction that, on returning to Japan, I deplaned and fought the urge to kiss the tarmac as if I had returned home, even though I stood halfway around the world from my actual home.

2. Actively pursue places where lost and broken people need help. God is always at work there.

It's wise to pray about where God is working and join Him there. Some of the stories you read in this book are living examples of that truth. God calls some of his field workers to other countries. He calls some to large or small ministries. And some He calls to minister in their own backyard. For example, in the story of Nehemiah and the rebuilding of the wall around Jerusalem after it had been nearly destroyed, some of the workers were positioned outside their own doors (read Nehemiah 3).

The Reverend Dr. Orlando Rivera, who died recently as a result of a car accident, understood this concept. When he and his wife purchased a large inner-city home, it wasn't only to house them and their children. Orlando and Nancy created an open-door policy to a safe haven. Children and adults alike knew they could walk up to the Riveras' door any time for a hot meal or a place to hang out. Orlando did his best preaching in his home. Anyone who came to the Riveras' could count on not only hearing the gospel but also hearing it told well. They'd located their calling by understanding a need God wanted to meet.

3. Don't let money make your decision.

Live below your means so you can be available when God calls you. There's nothing worse than a person stuck inside the city gates because of debt.

When we started out as a married couple, we pinched every penny. We committed to debtless living and attacked our mortgage aggressively, sending every spare cent to retiring the principal, something we accomplished in eight years. This positioned us to be open to the call of God. I took one job even though I didn't know how much I'd be paid until I received my first paycheck.

The issue wasn't money; it was destiny. That particular call was to a church as its youth pastor and as a high school supervisor for a private church school. I left a promising, growing private counseling practice because we felt God's leading. One day it seemed the devil himself walked into that tiny high-school portable building behind the church and said, "Look at you. Hidden back here in this metal box with fifteen teenagers, you're making much less than you're worth. Is this what you call following the will of God?" When I looked up from my tiny plastic desk, a student was working hard on a test. I knew enough about him to realize he desperately needed a positive male role model in his life. "Yes," I replied silently, "I am following the will of God."

4. Pay attention to the little leadings and relationships God orchestrates in your life.

My wife and I rented a garage apartment to a Christian woman. We talked regularly about her brother, who ran a family-policy council in our state. He was a driven, busy man who was passionate about marriage and children. One day she told me he was looking for someone to drive him around the state in a "get out the vote" campaign that targeted family issues. I felt led to volunteer. The hours in his car sealed a friendship that led to the two of us serving together on the Trail Life USA Board of Directors, where he is still the chairman.

I met Eva Marie Everson, who wrote this book with me, at a writers conference, where I signed up for her writing practicum. I shared some strategies regarding a tense situation she had with state custody of a child. This connection led to us co-directing a number of writers conferences and co-leading Word Weavers International, a ministry for Christian writers.

Be sensitive to these leadings because a seemingly temporary thread of a connection can be tied to a rope that bears eternal purpose.

STORIES OF THOSE
WHO LEFT THE GATE

EVELYN MIRACLE'S STORY

The core question: Does God really want me to marry this man and become a missionary?

What motivated you to action? After only one year of college, I became engaged to Mic, and we were planning to join the staff of Teen Missions International (TMI). Mic was scheduled to lead a team to Honduras while I worked in the TMI office. We figured a fall wedding would allow us time to raise support. I was packing for the trip when Mic walked into my house with a serious expression on his face. "Do you want to go to Florida as my fiancée or as my wife?"

What did you do? My jaw dropped, and I wondered whom he'd been talking to. All the practical barriers still loomed—no place to live and no money to live on for starters. I jumped on board his plan for a quickie wedding. We broke the news to our parents who weren't even surprised at our spontaneity. Three days later, we said our "I dos" in a lovely church wedding, followed by a drive to the Teen Missions headquarters.

We survived on wedding money that summer. The TMI director, Bob Bland, added me to the Honduras team, and my passport arrived only days before we flew out. My husband was in his element leading a group of teenagers to construct a school. I soon realized that our marriage was key to his response to God's call. My call was to go where he went, to serve with him no matter what.

What have been the results? During our first six years of marriage, my husband and I worked on the staff of Teen Missions. Every summer we led groups of teenagers to various places around the globe—Honduras, Mexico, France, Senegal, and Brazil. Not only were we building physical structures, but we also were building teens. Some of them became full-time missionaries; others became pastors and teachers. We never heard from most of them after they entered adulthood. We won't know the extent of our influence on them until we get to heaven.

I'll never forget the thrill of doing things I never dreamed I could do—such as cooking for a team of thirty-five in the Amazon jungle of Brazil. The most remote and difficult team became the one I most cherished. In spite of my fears, I helped lead that team with my husband. We successfully completed an airstrip that summer, and it's probably still in use by Wycliffe Bible Translators.

What would've happened if you hadn't responded to the call? I can't imagine my life if I had stayed in the little farming community where I grew up. If I hadn't said yes to my man and agreed to his invitation to go immediately, I would've missed so many of God's blessings. He stretched me way out of my comfort zone. I had to grow up and be a responsible adult when I was barely nineteen. I faced my fears of the unknown and learned to trust God to meet our needs. Anything God accomplished through me was by His grace. I was so inexperienced in the beginning. God could've used someone older and more experienced, but He chose me. My willingness mattered most.

Any regrets? We recently celebrated our forty-fourth wedding anniversary. Saying yes to my husband so many years ago meant I was saying yes to God, and I have no regrets. He planted us in Florida and allowed us to travel on mission trips around the world in the early years of our marriage. We remained here, raised three kids, and now we are grandparents. What a great foundation God laid for our family.

BRANDY HOPKINS' STORY

The core question: Is there something more I should be doing? My friend and I had seen the problem of mean girls in our youth group, and we knew the issue went way beyond our church walls. There are mean girls everywhere. Sadly, it isn't limited to one certain age. We also have daughters. The goal is to teach girls their worth in Jesus as well as to open the eyes of the mean girls and direct them to Jesus.

What motivated you to action? There's always something more we can do in all areas of our lives. I have to be aware of my limitations and discern what the Spirit is specifically calling my ministry partner and me to do. I have to focus on His call to the point that nothing can detour me.

What did you do? We began with what we thought would be a one-time slumber party for girls, showing them the love of Jesus. As we prayed about this event, the Lord expanded our vision and opened our eyes to what else we could do for young girls. We took our slumber-party concept and turned it into a conference. This conference is free to all girls; we raise our support. The conference includes, but is not limited to, a T-shirt, CD, packet of material, endless food, guest speakers, concert, fun, lots of Jesus and love. The conference celebrated its tenth anniversary in 2018.

What have been the results? This is what keeps me going: (1) when a girl comes to me and tells me that she's had the best day of her life; (2) getting late night calls from girls in crisis because they know that they can trust me (our leaders give all girls their phone numbers); (3) when I go to a public sports event and see girls wearing conference T-shirts with Bible verses on them; (4) when some girls accept Jesus for the first time and others rededicate their lives to Him. Friendships have also evolved from our conferences. It's very encouraging to see the girls on social media lifting up one another in prayer and support. These bonds are strong and they last.

I've been challenged in many ways throughout the years of heading this ministry. From pressing on during personal tragedy to wholly trusting the Lord for the resources, I've learned much. Anytime you work for the Lord, the Enemy doesn't like it. Therefore, he'll do anything to drag you down, wear you out, and test your faith. My faith has been stretched, tested, and practiced in ways that have drawn me closer to the Lord.

What would've happened if you hadn't responded to the call? On a greater scale, someone else eventually would've answered that call. However, the tragedy would be the girls with whom I had direct contact that may not have gotten the opportunity of going to the conference. I would not have experienced the relationships with others who share the heart for young girls as I do. I would not have had all the opportunities to stretch my faith.

Any regrets? None.

BRYAN DAVIS' STORY

The core question: Am I making a long-term impact for God? At the end of my life, will people be closer to God because of what I did during my lifetime?

What motivated you to action? As a computer professional, I made the world a better place technologically speaking, but any spiritual impact I had on people was limited to a tiny sphere of influence. I wanted to reach more people for God and do so in a way that would last for generations.

During those years of apparent futility, a question dogged my mind. I was writing a story about young people who faced great dangers, and yet they never shrank back. They always trusted God to see them through.

Was I doing the same? In my own journey to become an author, what risks was I taking? What would I lose if I never became an author?

What did you do? I pursued becoming an author. I read books on writing, attended critique group meetings, and went to writing conferences. Although I collected more than 200 rejections from publishers and agents, the passion to make an impact drove me onward.

Since I had a steady computer job, I wasn't taking any risks. I wasn't living out the faith that my fictional characters displayed. I was in danger of being a hypocrite.

What have been the results? I quit my job and pursued writing full time. My salary ended. Our liquid cash dwindled. We sold our dream home to make ends meet. Finally, a small publisher took a chance on my fantasy novel. When the book came out, I wondered if anyone would read the highly unusual story.

They did, beyond all my expectations. We have sold more than 500,000 copies of my inaugural series. I've received thousands of letters and emails from around the world—children who gained courage to face their fears, adults who reconciled with family members, elderly folks who can now look toward the afterlife without fear, and a multitude of teenagers who turned away from suicide and toward God.

This journey affected my own life as well. Months of uncertainty taught me how to trust God day by day. These experiences provided real-life lessons on how to be content in all situations and how to see God's sufficiency in all categories.

What would've happened if you hadn't responded to the call? I don't know what would've happened. Maybe God would've made more calls or led me in other ways. Maybe not. I do know that my stories have impacted thousands of readers in ways that will last for eternity. I also know that my own faith is stronger. I still rely on God day by day for everything, and I have peace. I'm doing exactly what God called me to do. I took the risks. I faced my fears. I trusted in God. I'm making an impact for Him.

Any regrets? I have no regrets.

JOE PUTTING'S STORY

The core question: My wife, Luanne, had been to China on a mission trip. It changed her life. She came home and told me we needed to adopt a child. I told her no and jokingly added, "I'll buy you an orphanage." Her next question, however, hit me to the core. Her challenge was clear: "Joe, why are we here? What's our purpose on earth? Is it only to do theatrical ministry or to discuss where we're going to eat? Or are we going all in?"

Over time, God made it clear in my prayer time that I shouldn't ask Him for anything else until I rescued a child. Initially, I was taken aback and uncomfortable. Luanne and I were on the verge of being empty nesters. But the truth became apparent: Luanne and I could raise more children. We'd raised two biological children who were well-adjusted, Christian young adults. What I didn't know was how we'd pay for the adoptions. I wrestled with God over that. He won.

What motivated you to action? Luanne and I knew thousands of orphans were out there. We knew what the Bible says about orphans in James 1:27: *Pure and undefiled religion before God and the Father is this: to visit orphans and widows in their trouble.* We couldn't help everyone, but we were certain we could help one.

What did you do? We did the paperwork and completed all the other requirements, then waited about a year for the red tape to untangle. Finally, in 2006 we traveled to Beijing, China, to pick up our adopted daughter who was just shy of her second birthday. About a year later, we found ourselves in Ethiopia adopting brother and sister, Hana and Jacob, who were elementary age.

What have been the results? Three lives were rescued and three souls were saved. Over the years, this family expansion has enabled us to build relationships with people involved in our children's schools and sports and elsewhere in the community. The fact that our family is multi-racial helps us connect easily with those of all races.

Today, all our adopted family members are committed Christians. Alisha is twelve, she's in middle school, and she's actively serving in the student ministry at church. Hana and Jacob, who didn't even know how to speak English when they arrived, have graduated from high school. They have enjoyed occasional visits to their homeland over the years, allowing them to maintain close relationships with their extended family. In fact, Hana recently returned from a three-month stint serving as a missionary in an orphanage in the Ethiopian village where she was born.

My hope is that our family has, in a small way, helped to tear down racial divides in our community, church, and around the world. Who knows what God will do in and through these children in the future?

What would've happened if you hadn't responded to the call? Definitely, my three adopted children would've grown up under drastically different circumstances. I cringe at the thought. Perhaps one or more would be starving. Maybe one or more would be addicted or trapped in prostitution. I can say for certain that they wouldn't be changing the world.

Any regrets? The only regret I have is that I didn't think of it myself. Seriously, in my preaching over the last thirty years, I've often asked one question: What does faith really look like in your life?

To be honest, there aren't many instances in an American Christian's life that faith really and truly must be exercised, due to the comfort level we enjoy in our nation. Exceptions would be a loved one's death, a life-threatening diagnosis, divorce, and other instances of profound grief. During these challenges, our faith sustains us and can prevent us from harmful choices we might otherwise make if we try to grapple with grief on our own.

Aside from those personal trials, what I've learned is that in America a leap of faith always seems to involve money—more specifically, it involves parting

152

with it. To be honest, that was where my faith was challenged. But God won me over. While the decision to adopt and raise three orphans has been a serious financial investment and, at times, a very wild ride, it has been a spiritual journey and a sweet experience of blessings I'll never forget or regret.

Adoption showed me what real-life faith looks like. I've had a front-row seat for watching what God can do in and through my three adopted children and those they impact.

As time has passed, Luanne and I have shared our faith experience with others, and it has rubbed off on them. Several couples in the church and the community have followed our example, adopting children from our area and all over the world.

A few years ago we launched a ministry, Bringing Children Home, to assist members of our church family who need help with adoption costs. Meanwhile, as a church family, we've stepped up our financial commitment to orphanages locally and globally through mission efforts that touch lives for Jesus in every nation of the world.

CINDIE THOMAS' STORY

The core question: If I can do this for a few, can I do it for more than a few?

What motivated you to action? I'd felt God nudging me for years to become a spokesperson and advocate for the unborn. In the '70s, I participated in the pro-life movement in my hometown, and I'd always felt the tug on my heart to be a voice for those who have no voice. The daughters of several friends had unplanned pregnancies, and I'd counseled them not to abort. Thank God they chose life. Then came a time in my life when I could take the training required to become a volunteer at the Sanford Pregnancy Center. So I did.

I am motivated by knowing all life is a gift from God. Once, when I was a young child, my mother told me in a fit of anger that if abortions had been legal, she would've had one when she found herself pregnant with me. As a result, I wanted to offer hope to young women faced with unplanned pregnancies. Psalm 139:13 tells us that God knit us together in our mother's womb. This means we are not accidents.

What did you do? I volunteered at first and then became the director of a new center we started in Oviedo, Florida. I counseled young women and their families, directed them to available resources in our community, spoke at churches and women's groups, and helped with fund-raising.

What have been the results? The results have been amazing ... only God! One woman I helped now attends a local church, attends a Bible study, has her own apartment, has received several promotions at work, has both her driver's license and a car, and takes online classes through a Bible college. She has been reunited with her mother and has had the blessing of meeting the daughter she gave up for adoption. If she were the only one I'd helped, the experience would've been worth every moment.

One of the biggest impacts for me personally was ministering to a young woman who was a crack addict and a prostitute on the streets of Sanford. Getting to know her, seeing the pain and sadness in her life changed me and my life. Before I worked at the center, I saw her on the streets—high on drugs and sometimes acting pretty wild. I wondered why she couldn't straighten herself out. When I met her face-to-face at the center, I had a heart transformation. I thought of my own life. I could've been that girl on the street. My daughter could've been on the street. This woman was not only someone's daughter; she was also the daughter of the King of Kings.

After she got out of jail for, I believe, the twenty-eighth time, she chose rehab, and I helped raise money to keep her there. After a few months, a volunteer's husband offered her a job.

What would've happened if you hadn't responded to the call? If I hadn't responded, I don't think I ever would've developed the compassion and understanding I now have for both young women faced with unplanned pregnancies and those addicted to drugs. Truly life changing.

Any regrets? I have no regrets at all.

EVA MARIE EVERSON'S STORY

The core question: Will you do this for Me, even if I don't do for you what you'd hoped?

What motivated you to action? For nearly twenty years, I worked hard as a writer to make it—whatever that meant. In the opening years, I had visions of grandeur. We all do, I think, if we're honest. I wanted to be a best-selling author. I wanted book tours with scads of fans wrapped around the bookstores, waiting with book in hand for my autograph. I wanted to be respected by my colleagues. I wanted one book (although I'd settle for many) that defined who I was as an artist.

In the early years, I helped form a small group of writers who wanted to help each other. Iron sharpening iron, we said. As the group grew, then faltered, God showed me a path that would lead to success for the group—not only as a group but also for the writers individually. I took the role of president of Word Weavers, located in Orlando, Florida, although we drew writers from all over the state.

Then, after fifteen years of growth, something amazing happened. We had founded chapters not only across the United States but also in other countries. Word Weavers International was formed. It needed a leader devoted to it, and I wasn't sure I was that person. Then came my wrestling match with God. He wanted my complete devotion, and that meant tuning my talents to the dial of other writers, especially beginners.

What did you do? I increased my presence at writers conferences and spent most of my days sharpening the craft of new and intermediate writers. This included taking on editing and coaching jobs as well as working as a managing editor at a small publishing house whose intent was to help talented writers who weren't receiving the attention they deserved from larger houses. I also signed contracts to work with new writers as a "with" author (such as this book).

What have been the results? The results have been the greatest blessing. Isn't it amazing what happens when we stop fighting with God? As in the story of Jacob and his night of wrestling with God (Genesis 32: 22–32), the only thing that happens when you find yourself in the same position is that God wins and you walk away with a limp. Not only have I watched those I've worked with go on to publication, but I've also cheered as they won countless awards and accolades.

As for Word Weavers International, in the few years since I decided to let God have His way, I've watched it grow from about 350 members to 650 members, with membership growing at thrilling rate. These writers have predominately one goal: write to advance the mission of God's kingdom, to see God's children drawn to His heart, and to prepare for the return of Messiah Jesus.

But God didn't forget me. One novel shot up to number one in the CBA bestseller list (fiction), and the following novel was named one of the top ten works of inspirational fiction for 2017 by BookList. Here's the strange thing—seeing others succeed has become my greatest prize. Now who would've thought that twenty years ago?

What would've happened if you hadn't responded to the call? I don't believe for one second that God's work would've been thwarted. Someone would've heeded the call, but it wouldn't have been me. God would've received the glory, and I would've missed out on the joy.

Any regrets? Not a single one.

ENDNOTES

1 Genesis 3:9
2 Mark 8:29
3 John 5:6
4 Matthew 7:13
5 2 Kings 6:27
6 2 Kings 7:3
7 2 Kings 7:4
8 2 Kings 7:5
9 2 Kings 7:6
10 2 Kings 6:25
11 2 Kings 6:28
12 2 Kings 7:1
13 2 Kings 7:2
14 Matthew 25:14–28 and Luke 19:11–27
15 John 10:10
16 Galatians 5:22
17 Ephesians 3:20
18 1 Chronicles 12:23
19 1 Chronicles 12:1–40
20 1 Chronicles 12:32 (ESV)
21 Matthew 11:12
22 Matthew 10:16
23 Romans 8:11

[24] John 21:5 (ESV)
[25] John 21:6 (ESV)
[26] Genesis 8:22
[27] 1 Chronicles 14:14–16
[28] Romans 10:17
[29] Exodus 2:15
[30] Psalm 90:12
[31] 2 Kings 7:5
[32] Luke 15:17
[33] Luke 15:20
[34] Ecclesiastes 3:1
[35] Psalm 23:3
[36] 1 Samuel 17:28–29
[37] John 8:32–36
[38] Psalm 118:6
[39] Luke 6:19
[40] Luke 9:1–2
[41] Romans 8:11
[42] John 14:12
[43] 1 John 3:8
[44] 1 John 3:9
[45] 1 John 1:2–3
[46] 2 Corinthians 5:20
[47] Passion 2010
[48] John 10:2–4
[49] Genesis 1:28
[50] Genesis 3:1

51 Romans 10:14

52 John 8:7

53 2 Corinthians 5:18–19

54 Translated: "I need a boat."

55 1 Corinthians 1:27–29

56 The story of Gideon begins in Judges 6.

57 Judges 6:36–40

58 See Judges 7:4–7

59 See Exodus 1:8

60 Joseph's story begins in Genesis 37 and concludes
   in Genesis 50.

61 Exodus 4:1–2

62 Exodus 4:3

63 Ephesians 1:3–6

64 Hebrews 11:6

65 Mark 16:15

66 Romans 8:11

67 Colossians 1:27

68 "Respect," Merriam-Webster, https://www.merri-
   am-webster.com/dictionary/respect.

69 1 Corinthians 6:19

70 "Self-esteem," Merriam-Webster, http://www.dic-
   tionary.com/browse/self-esteem?s=t.

71 Jeremiah 17:9

72 Jeremiah 17:10

73 Isaiah 29:16

74 2 Kings 7:9

[75] Psalm 139:13

[76] Ephesians 2:10

[77] Genesis 1:28

[78] Genesis 3:1

[79] John 19:30

[80] Revelation 16:17

[81] Proverbs 15:23

[82] Matthew 26:63

[83] 1 Peter 2:22–23

[84] "Edwin Louis Cole Quotes," BrainyQuote, https://www.brainyquote.com/quotes/edwin_louis_cole_360099.

[85] Psalm 62:1–2

[86] Isaiah 64:6

[87] Mark 4:35

[88] Mark 4:36

[89] Matthew 26:40–45

[90] Acts 1:1

[91] Mark 5:1–20

[92] Romans 10:14

[93] Matthew 11:30

[94] John 4:34

[95] Colossians 1:24–27

[96] 2 Kings 7:4

[97] Proverbs 4:18

[98] Edwin Louis Cole, *Entering and Leaving Crisis: A Step by Step Guide for Times of Transition*, (Tulsa, OK: Al-

bury Publishing, 1998)

99   Romans 8:28

100   1 John 1:1–4

101   Sermon given at Northland, a Church Distributed. Words are approximate based on one of the author's notes.

102   John 4:35

103   Matthew 28:19

104   C.H. Spurgeon, "Public Testimony: A Debt to God and Man," sermon no. 1996 in *The Complete Works of C. H. Spurgeon*, Volume 33: Sermons 1938–2000. (Delmarva Publications, 2013), Google Books.

105   Exodus 5:1

106   Paraphrased from Exodus 3–4

107   Exodus 12:37

108   The parable of the talents is recorded in both Matthew 25 and Luke 19. The passage quoted is Matthew 25:14–18.

109   Mark 4:35

110   Habakkuk 2:2

111   Exodus 4:2

112   Psalm 34:18

If you'd like a free downloadable group study guide for *Why Are We Sitting Here Until We Die?* or if you'd like to find out more about Mark T. Hancock or Trail Life USA, go to www.MarkTHancock.com.

Made in the USA
Monee, IL
17 May 2023